26 IUMAR 1970.

D0313934

Unsolved Murders in Victorian and Edwardian London

Unsolved Murders in Victorian and Edwardian London

JONATHAN OATES

RBWM LIBRARY SERVICES

Wharncliffe Books

First Published in Great Britain in 2007 by
Wharncliffe Books
an imprint of
Pen and Sword Books Ltd
47 Church Street
Barnsley
South Yorkshire
S70 2AS

Copyright © Jonathan Oates 2007

ISBN: 978-184563-045-4

The right of Jonathan Oates to be identified as the author
of this work has been asserted by her in accordance with
the Copyright, Designs and Patents Act 1988.

A CIP catalogue record for this book is available from the
British Library.

All rights reserved. No part of this publication may be
reproduced, stored in a retrieval system, or transmitted, in
any form or by any means, electronic, mechanical,
photocopying, recording or otherwise, without the prior
permission in writing of the publishers.

Typeset in 10/12pt Plantin by Concept, Huddersfield.

Printed and bound in England by CPI UK.

Pen and Sword Books Ltd incorporates the Imprints of
Pen & Sword Aviation, Pen & Sword Maritime,
Pen & Sword Military, Wharncliffe Books,
Pen & Sword Select, Pen and Sword Military Classics
and Leo Cooper.

For a complete list of Pen & Sword titles please contact
PEN & SWORD BOOKS LIMITED
47 Church Street
Barnsley
South Yorkshire
S70 2BR
England
E-mail: enquiries@pen-and-sword.co.uk
Website: www.pen-and-sword.co.uk

Contents

Acknowledgements

My thanks go the many archivists and librarians who have answered my questions about their holdings and who have brought me a myriad number of documents and books which provide the source material for this book. My thanks also go to those who have allowed me to use postcards from their collections; namely John Coulter, and Reg Eden of the West London Postcard Collectors' Club. My wife accompanied me in taking the modern photographs seen here. Mike Egan, Kidbrooke's historian, kindly commented on two chapters. I also need to extend my thanks to my predecessors – those whose works are cited in the bibliography. Without their work on murders solved and unsolved, the number of unsolved murders here would have been far fewer. I may not always have agreed with their conclusions or even their facts, but their work has certainly guided mine. I would also like to thank Mr John Gauss for looking through the script for English and grammar errors. Finally, the Metropolitan Police supplied me with statistics about more recent murders.

Any factual accuracies, are of course, mine alone.

This book is dedicated to Tony, who disapproves.

Introduction

D r Watson wrote about Sherlock Holmes's investigations thus: 'Some, and not the least interesting, were complete failures, and as such will hardly bear narrating, since no final explanation is forthcoming. A problem without a solution may interest the student, but can hardly fail to annoy the casual reader.' All the cases of real life crime narrated here fall into this category, but it does not mean they are unworthy of study or uninteresting.

Indeed, there is a fascination in unsolved murder that outweighs that which has been solved. If the man (or woman) on the proverbial Clapham omnibus was asked to name a Victorian murderer, most would give one name, or rather, pseudonym: Jack the Ripper. That his crimes were horrific there is no doubt, but why choose him? This unknown man was in no ways the most prolific killer in British history – Dr Shipman earns that dubious accolade. Then there is Peter Sutcliffe, the 'Yorkshire Ripper'. Reginald Christie probably killed more than the Whitechapel murderer, and yet he is hardly a household name, despite his misdeeds being far more recent.

The reason why he is well known is that the numerous books, films and TV series about him keep him in the public eye (or, rather, his crimes). Numerous theories about his identity have been propounded over the past century. They have included a Polish Jew, a Liverpool businessman, a Russian doctor, a barrister, a prince, an American eccentric, a poisoner, a royal doctor – the list is a long one. There is a horror and a fascination in unsolved crime, especially unsolved murder. Who was responsible and why did they commit such terrible deeds? In fact, unsolved crime, if of sufficient age, becomes a form of parlour game. Everyone can have their own theory and the 'game' need have no end as it is unsolvable. Yet the Ripper was not the only killer who got away with his crimes. Many others did so. Why was this?

This book looks at over a score of unsolved murders in Victorian and Edwardian London (1837–1914). Most were in central London, such as the remains of the body found on Waterloo Bridge in 1857, and in Battersea, Lambeth, Whitechapel, and the West End, and a few in the leafy suburbs, such as Eltham in 1871, when a pregnant girl was viciously killed. Two murders occurred on trains. Most of these murders have been covered in books about London crimes, but almost all are unknown to the general public. The exception is Jack the Ripper, but rather than compress this well- known tale into one chapter, I have decided to look at just two of his crimes – and they may not have been committed by him at all. It does not cover every single killing, due to want of space – Mrs Samuel was killed in 1878, Emma Smith in 1888 and an unknown woman in the following year, and there were many others whose slayers remain unknown. For a partial list, see the appendix at the back of the book.

The number of killings was low by contemporary standards. There were 198 murders, which include abortions (about 10 per cent of the total), in 1896–1905 (which compares favourably to the 475 from January 2004 to September 2006). Of the earlier murders, 19 were unsolved. At the time of writing, no one had been charged with 72 of the modern murders, though in most cases investigations are ongoing.

Each chapter will describe a crime, follow the initial investigation, the inquest, examine the suspects, if any, and conclude with that which seems probable. Even so, none of these chapters, by necessity, can have a definitive and conclusive ending. I have also discussed various theories which previous writers have aired. The reader will have to make up their own mind, based on the evidence before them and their own reading of the events and people described therein. I have suggested possibilities and questions which need answering, though have not always, or even often, answered them.

It is always tempting, though, to speculate on the identity of the killer. However, real life is not the same as detective fiction, where the killer is almost always one of a circle of characters all of whom are known to the detective and the reader. So, though we may consider one of the known characters as being the possible killer, in the case of these real murders, the real murderer was probably someone completely unknown to the police and whose name never cropped up in their investigations (Jack the Ripper probably falls into this category).

In claiming these murders are unsolved, I do not mean to say that they are unsolvable. What is meant is that no one was ever convicted of having been responsible. Possibly more information may come to light, though at this late date it seems improbable. There are a few cases in which a suspect was tried at the Old Bailey, but was acquitted. Whether that acquittal was necessarily the right verdict is another question – in 1907, for example, the police thought that the accused man had killed one Phyllis Dimmock, but the jury found him not guilty, nonetheless.

In finding the cases which appear in this book, I have read numerous books about murders in London. They tend to concentrate on quantity and include the solved murders (the majority), too, and so can only allot a few paragraphs to each. Here is far more detail. Furthermore, about a quarter of the crimes detailed here have, to the

London Bridge, c.1906. Reg Eden's collection

best of my knowledge, never been discussed in print since the press reports at the time they were committed.

The evidence for this book has been taken from contemporary sources – those written at the time of the murders and shortly afterwards. These include the files of the Metropolitan Police held at the National Archives. They contain statements by witnesses, police officers and police surgeons. There is not such a file for every murder here; in fact only about half of those chronicled are covered by them. Conspiracy theorists writing about the Whitechapel murders often insist that files have been deliberately suppressed or destroyed in order to conceal the crimes of the high born, but there is no need to heed such theories. In fact there are files on all the Ripper victims but often nothing on some of the other cases chronicled here. Records can be destroyed haphazardly and those that survive often do so as a matter of luck. Some files are incomplete.

Where the official files do not exist, and even where they do, the contemporary press has been used, and though this is probably not the most reliable source, it is the only other which remains to us. *The Times*, in particular, had extensive coverage of murder cases in London in the nineteenth century, especially those which came to trial. And finding material is now fairly easy because of *The Times* on-line digital archive. Local newspapers, such as the *Middlesex County Times* and the *Kentish Mercury* have been examined, too, as has the *Illustrated Police News*.

The City of London, centre of global finance, c.1904. Reg Eden's collection

It should be recalled, however, that most murders in London were solved. As Sir Robert Anderson, head of the CID in 1888, noted in his memoirs, 'I may say that "undiscovered murders" are rare in London'. He added that between 1903 and 1908, there had been ninety-two murders in the capital (population *c.*7 million) and, if four (illegal) abortions are excluded all but six were solved.

The ones which appear here are, therefore, very much the exception. Even so, as *The Times* observed in 1873, this was largely by default:

> *The discovery of ordinary murders is the result of the hurry or the short-sightedness of those who commit them, rather than any preternatural sagacity that is brought to bear upon the enquirer; and it is both conceivable, and within the range of experience, that a murderer whose plans have been well laid should not only escape detection, but that he should even escape suspicion.*

Henry Adam, in his *Police Encyclopedia* of 1914 further noted:

> *When a murder is committed for which nobody is arrested and convicted, it is universally supposed that the police are, in a greater or lesser degree, answerable for such an unsatisfactory state of things. This, however, is by no means the case, for they may be quite confident as to by whom the crime has been committed, but unable to effect an arrest in consequence of the limitations of the laws of evidence.*

The author has had two books about different districts of London published in 'The Foul Deeds and Suspicious Deaths' series and so is knowledgeable about crime in the capital's bloody past.

A note on money

In those pre-decimal days, before 1971, Britain's currency was thus:

4 farthings or 2 halfpennies = 1 penny (abbreviated to d).
12 pennies = 1 shilling (abbreviated to s).
20 shillings = 1 pound (note) or 1 sovereign (coin).
1 pound and 1 shilling = 1 guinea.

In 1902, a working man might have an income of £75 per year (a female worker would expect far less), a middle-class professional perhaps about £200–£400 and a member of the upper class over £5,000.

CHAPTER 1

Policing the Capital in the Victorian and Edwardian Eras

Any man of average stature and strength may wander about on foot and alone, at any hour of the day or night ... and never have so much as the thought of any danger thrust upon him.

Befo re reading the cases of unsolved crimes, we need to recall those who had the task of investigating them. What was the nineteenth- and early twentieth-century police force like, and what were their strengths and weaknesses?

When Queen Victoria ascended the throne in 1837, the Metropolitan Police was still a relatively recent innovation. In 1829 the revolutionary step had been taken to create the Metropolitan Police – the first time that a uniformed civilian body of men had existed to deter and detect crime in London. It was founded by Sir Robert Peel, the reforming Tory Home Secretary, and was initially only 3,000 strong, split into seventeen divisions and covering seven square miles. In 1840 the Metropolitan area in which they worked was expanded to cover rural Middlesex, northern Surrey and Kent and the western extremes of Essex. It was divided into twenty-two districts. Each district was given an initial letter – the H district covered the East End, for example. Each of these districts was under the care of a superintendent. He would have command over inspectors, sergeants and constables in the police stations in that district (several hundred men in all). A civilian doctor was co-opted as the divisional police surgeon and would examine any murder victims.

Overall control of the Metropolitan Police went not to any elected local body but to the government, in the form of the Home Secretary. He appointed a Police Commissioner to exercise day-to-day control of the capital's police. Senior police officers did not have to work their way up through the ranks. Colonel Charles Rowan, who had served under Wellington, was the first Commissioner and Sir Charles Warren, Commissioner between 1886 and 1888 and in overall charge of the Ripper investigation, had also been a soldier.

The police were uniformed in long blue coats, black top hats and white trousers. This was to differentiate them from the army, who wore red coats. In 1864 they began to wear blue tunics and helmets. They carried truncheons, though other weapons could be issued. Rattles, and later, whistles, were carried to summon help from colleagues. Their role was to patrol the streets and deter crime. If crime occurred, they then had to apprehend the perpetrators. They also had to patrol political demonstrations, such as the huge Chartist rallies in the 1840s and the Hyde Park meetings two decades later. By 1900, the force numbered nearly 16,000 men and they patrolled nearly 700 square miles. There were no policewomen in this period, of course.

Towards the end of the nineteenth century there were fresh challenges. These included Irish terrorists and militant unionists. In the early years of the twentieth century, anarchists, Communists, Suffragettes and German spies were all real or imagined dangers which stretched police resources. Metropolitan police were also dispatched to other parts of the country when the need arose, chiefly to deter rioting.

It eventually became the sole task of the Criminal Investigation Department (CID) to investigate serious crime. The detective branch was formed in 1842, with only eight detectives, rising to fifteen in 1868. It was only in 1878 that the CID was formed and the two branches of the police force were separated. The uniformed force would call upon the detective branch when a crime had to be investigated.

Initially the police faced many problems. One was that they were unpopular. Many people, not only criminals or political radicals, saw them as a dangerous threat to civil liberty, as well as adding to the burden of taxation. They were seen as the agents of the government, not impartial officers preserving law and order. The police were accused of brutality in using violence to break up demonstrations (such as the Trafalgar Square riots in 1887, known as Bloody Sunday to some, where two men later died), though it should be recalled that protesters were not adverse to using violence, either. Many officers were killed in the course of duty – two constables were killed in Deptford in the 1830s and 1840s. The constables were known as Peelers, Bobbies, Peel's 'Blue Devils' and, most offensively of all, pigs. Sympathy for these men was often minimal. When PC Cull was killed in a riot in 1833, the jury returned a verdict of justifiable homicide and there were annual celebratory banquets in subsequent

Scotland Yard. John Coulter's collection

years. Furthermore, policemen were occasionally not adverse to corrupt and criminal practices themselves. In the 1870s, a major scandal damaged the reputation of the detective force, as it was discovered that the detectives had been accepting bribes from the very criminals they were meant to suppress. The culprits were dismissed from the force.

The calibre of the officers was also variable, and this did not help their image. There was a fairly high turnover of manpower because many men had to be dismissed due to drunkenness. Within four years of their being founded, only one in six of the original men was still in the ranks. The fact that pay was low (3 shillings a day; not much above that of a labourer), hours were long and the work could be dangerous and unsociable deterred many men from joining. Many former soldiers joined at first, giving the force a reputation of being militaristic, reinforced by the fact that many senior officers had army backgrounds.

By the early twentieth century, police complaints grew. Pensions were not granted until 1890. Apart from low pay and low status, until 1910 they had to work seven days a week, complaining 'even convicts are allowed time for recreation'. Although it was not until 1919 that there were to be police strikes, such was the frustration and militancy of the rank and file of the constabulary, morale was poor throughout much of the period under survey.

It was only towards the end of the nineteenth century that the police became less controversial and more widely accepted. Even then, popular detective stories were not particularly complimentary towards them. Witness Sherlock Holmes telling Watson in *A Study in Scarlet* (1887) about Messrs Lestrade and Gregson 'the pick of a bad bunch' and the same novel depicts Constable John Rance as a figure of ridicule, too. Inspector Hopkins is deemed worthy of praise, but even he needs Holmes's help. The press was also often hostile because police officers did not divulge information about investigations to reporters – for fear that such would assist the criminals.

Yet the police had had some success. A Victorian historian wrote of the 1870s that:

> *Any man of average stature and strength may wander about on foot and alone, at any hour of the day or night, through the greatest of all cities and its suburbs, along the high roads, and through unfrequented country lanes, and never have so much as the thought of any danger thrust upon him, unless he goes out of his way to court it.*

An Italian visitor to London claimed that the policeman did not need to use his weapon because 'on hearing a policeman's voice nobody answers and everybody obeys like a lamb', though this is certainly an exaggeration. Lawlessness, in terms of recorded offences fell, there being fewer offences committed in 1900 than 1830, despite the fact that population had soared between those dates.

The police force had relatively few scientific aids until the end of the nineteenth century. Forensic science was still in its infancy. Fingerprinting was not used until the 1890s and it was in 1905 that fingerprints were first used to convict killers in Deptford. A detective training school was founded in 1902. As late as 1888 it was believed that the retina of the eyes of a murder victim could be photographed in order to show who the killer was. There were no tests for identifying bloodstains in this period. Of course, there was no such thing as DNA evidence then, either.

Methods of detection were limited. Unless a criminal was caught in the act or shortly afterwards, it could be difficult to catch them. Confessions, though, were not uncommon, providing a suspect could be found. But to convict a criminal on evidence alone was very difficult, unless there were reliable witnesses and murder is not usually committed in front of an audience. Police work was usually painstaking, but was rarely scientific until the end of the period chronicled here. There was a lack of innovation and imagination; often a single line of enquiry was followed to the exclusion of everything else.

The way in which murder investigations were carried out in the Victorian era seem very haphazard in the harsh light of hindsight. The

A London Policeman directs traffic, c.1910. Author's collection

routine procedure was as follows. If a civilian made the find, he or she would usually call a policeman. This would probably be the nearest constable on his beat. Often, though, bodies were found by the beat constable, as in the cases of Alice McKenzie in 1889 and Frances Coles in 1891. Then the officer would summon a superior officer, a doctor (usually the divisional surgeon) and his colleagues – the latter by blowing his whistle. He would then stay with the body until others arrived. The doctor would pronounce life to be extinct and the corpse would be carted off to the mortuary. Blood and other substances, including, perhaps, important clues which might be located at the scene of the crime, would then be washed away. To take photographs of the crime scene was unusual. At the mortuary the clothes of the deceased would be discarded and thrown away (again, possibly discarding vital clues in the process), whilst the doctor examined the corpse to discover the cause of death. There was no careful investigation for the tiny clues; such as a hair or a piece of fabric which belonged to the killer, which would now help lead the police to the killer. There are a number of cases in this book where such tiny clues would have been critical in either identifying the criminal or proving conclusively that an innocent man was in the clear. The body would also be officially identified, usually by next of kin or a close friend of the deceased.

After this initial stage, an inquest would be held by the county coroner or his deputy in order to find the cause of death and where responsibility for it lay. A jury of twelve men, usually local, would be summoned, and they would meet in a public building; often a pub or a church hall. They would have to view the body. The doctor would give the cause of death and then it was usual for the inquest to be adjourned whilst the police located witnesses, clues and suspects.

Once the inquest was resumed, the witnesses would tell what they could about the deceased, often their last known movements, as well as the actual circumstances of finding the corpse. Policemen would usually be present, both as witnesses, and observers. Finally, the coroner would sum up the evidence and instruct the jury to come to a conclusion as to how the person died, and who, if anyone, was responsible. If there was a suspect that the jury pointed the finger at, he or she would then go before a magistrates' court, where they would be defended and witnesses brought forward to support their case. If they were still thought to be guilty, they would be tried before the Old Bailey, officially the Central Criminal Court, which dealt with all murder cases in London and its environs. Since murder was then a capital crime, the jury had a great responsibility and if there was reasonable doubt about the accused, they were instructed to acquit the prisoner. Yet most cases here did not reach this stage.

Rewards and informers had been a key part in the process of detection in the eighteenth century. Rewards for the apprehension of killers continued in the nineteenth century, but eventually were frowned upon. This was because it was thought that they encouraged informers and the planting of evidence upon the innocent. Even so, the system was popular with the public – the police were criticized for not offering rewards for the Ripper in 1888 until after several women had been killed. The problem was that rewards did not always work – especially when trying to catch a lone killer, who had no accomplice who could betray him.

It is important that the reader realizes that methods of detection were very primitive before they condemn the police too harshly. Luck played its part. Even with modern scientific methods, many criminals can escape justice at the beginning of the twenty-first century, too. One could argue that the police did well, so that unsolved murders were very much the minority, as noted earlier.

It is also worth pointing out that policing a capital city is difficult. Its very size and (often transient) population cause problems. London's population expanded rapidly between 1841 and 1911 from 1.9 million to 4.5 million (for greater London the figures were 2.2 million to 7.2 million). Furthermore, much of this expansion came from immigration. People arrived from all over the British Isles in search of work. Political refugees and others escaping persecution, such as Jews from Eastern Europe, settled in London. With such a transitional population, criminals could come and go with relative ease and the police had trouble tracking down such villains. Better transport links in and out of London also gave criminals greater mobility and the means to escape if need be.

It should be recalled that most killers and victims are well known to each other – as family members, friends or colleagues. These murders are relatively easy to solve and their motives are usually clear enough. But the murders of strangers – which most of those chronicled here appear to be – are far more difficult. Motives are thus hard to ascertain. A late Victorian senior police officer said that if a killer was not caught within twenty-four hours then he had probably got away with his misdeed, and there is much to be said for this generalization.

London was expanding throughout this period and its population was increasingly heterogeneous. The police force was not always popular and the men in the ranks not always happy. The methods at their disposal were relatively primitive. Is it any wonder, then, that some murderers escaped detection?

CHAPTER 2

The Death of a Barmaid
1837

*... he had the knife in his hand
when he went out, I am quite certain
of that, I saw it, it was bloody, as was
his hand.*

Miss Eliza Davis never had much luck in her short life. She was born in about 1816, but her parents died within weeks of each other whilst she was in her infancy. Her uncle, a small farmer in Montgomeryshire, looked after her for the next few years. When she was thirteen they sent her to London, having presumably already found her a job at the King's Arms, Frederick Street, which was owned by a Mr Berry and was just off the Hampstead Road. She was able to save a portion of her wages in a bank and by the age of twenty-one, the young barmaid had accumulated £23, which means she must have spent very little money. Unfortunately, the morning of Tuesday 9 May 1837 was to be her last.

As usual, Eliza rose early. Taking the keys from her master, she unlocked the pub and so it was open for business before anyone else in the place had stirred. At 6.20 pm, a workman by the name of Hall was passing and, seeing the door open, came in for a pint of beer. He was a regular customer and was surprised that he could not see anyone, so called out. Then he saw that the floor behind the bar was bloody. He raised his voice and attracted the attention of Jones, the potboy, who, only partially dressed, came down the stairs. Then he almost stumbled.

He had not seen Eliza's body, her throat cut, on the landing behind the bar, about six steps up. Her death must have been very recent because the corpse was still warm. They then called the police. There was no robbery or sexual assault, nor had there been any attempt at either. A bloodstained knife was found on the bar, and there was also a half-empty glass of beer and a penny piece there. Bloodstains were found on the handle of the door which led out to the west side of the pub.

Hampstead Road, 2006. The street where the King's Arms once stood was near here.
Author's collection

Inspector Aggs and PC Pegler of S division investigated the murder. Dr Swaine examined the corpse. This was, without doubt, a case of murder. He concluded:

> *That at the moment the act had been committed she must have been standing with her back to the bar, which is very narrow, across which her head had been drawn by the clump of hair behind, and the wound inflicted suddenly, with great force, and by one single action, which had separated the integuments, muscles, wind pipe and right carotid artery, down to the vertebus of the neck.*

There was also blood on her right hand, arm and on her bosom but very little on the floor or elsewhere. This was probably the result of Eliza trying to stem the flow of blood as soon as she had been attacked. Being unable to use her voice to sound the alarm, she had tried to warn the rest of the household by mounting the steps. Unfortunately, she had been unable to do so, and collapsed, due to loss of blood, on the first landing. Here she bled to death.

The public authorities were shocked by the crime and a reward of over £50 was announced for anyone who could identify the killer. Eliza was clearly a popular girl, for her employer paid for her funeral and a large crowd was expected at her burial on Sunday 14 May.

More macabre was a man taking a plaster cast of the deceased's face and the surgeons who queued up to see the corpse. Police were stationed at the pub, where the body lay, in order to prevent any disorder, such was the excitement that the murder generated locally, with hundreds congregating around it.

A number of witnesses came forward. The first was Mr Malpas, a butcher, who had been travelling past the pub on the morning of the murder, at about 5.40 am. He had seen a man standing near the pub and Malpas told him that it would not be open yet (despite the fact that licensing laws were very liberal at this time). The man made no reply and seemed deep in thought. Malpas walked past him, but was convinced he would know him again. He said that the man's description was as follows, 'five feet nine or ten inches high, rather thin, and wearing a black coat and fustian trousers'.

A more detailed description was issued and this was printed on reward posters. It read:

> 5 Feet 10 Inches High – of a Fair Complexion – pale Visage – rather thin and Athletic, and apparently from 28–30 Years of age – He wore a dark surtout Coat, very much worn, a double breasted dark striped waist-coat, a Fustian Trousers, and had about his Neck a Black silk Handkerchief; he said that he was a Modeller, and has the appearance of a working Mechanic. He is no Foreigner, as has been stated in some of the Papers.

Another witness was one James Gee, who saw a man in the vicinity of the scene of the crime washing his hands in a gutter. He was tall and wore a dark coat. This may well have been the killer who would have had bloodstained hands.

The landlord, Mr Wadley, thought the killer was a man who had been coming in for a drink early each morning. According to him, the man was 'an ill looking fellow', tall, thin, aged about thirty, wearing a blue coat, a Scottish plaid waistcoat, fustian trousers ands a white apron. The description was similar to that given above. He thought that a gypsy who had been hanging about the bar was responsible.

Although many men were suspected and some arrested, no one was convicted. Suspects included a Frenchman called Emtre, who had recently threatened Eliza. He may have been the foreigner who was arrested in Bath. Mr Hitchcock, a barman, claimed that a man had visited the pub a few days previously, but never afterwards, and Eliza had complained about his behaviour towards her. Another theory was that the landlord, who was unmarried, was the killer and had planted the penny, the knife and the half drunk glass of beer to throw the police off the scent. But this is mere supposition and there was no motive why he should do so. Eliza did not have a lover, so that avenue of enquiry could not be investigated. Over a dozen men were taken on suspicion, but none were identified by the witnesses. By the end of July, the active police investigation was called off, but it was not forgotten.

A few years later, other evidence came to light. In 1841, the governor of the House of Correction at St Albans, wrote to say that an inmate, David Venables, claimed to have important information about the case. Venables said that he had been walking in the vicinity of the pub on the morning of the crime and he met a man, one Henry McCane, who asked him to sharpen his knife on the grinder he was carrying, in return for a pint of beer. Venables did so.

McCane then went to the King's Arms and, according to Venables,

I saw him take the barmaid round the neck and cut her throat with the same knife I had ground for him, immediately he walked out of the house by the same door he had entered . . . he had the knife in his hand when he went out, I am quite certain of that, I saw it, it was bloody, as was his hand.

Venables then fled the scene. Yet the police did not believe the story, 'there is not the slightest doubt it [the murder] was done with a table knife belonging to the house, and which was found lying bloody on the bar'. Furthermore, Venables said the killer left by the southern door, whereas it had been by the western door. Although McCane was 'as bad as any in London' – both he and Venables had spent time in custody, the police concluded there was not 'the slightest reason to suspect him'. It was probably a case of one criminal falling out with another and then trying to incriminate him.

In the following year, a resident of Jersey contacted the police with news that he knew someone who was knowledgeable about the murder. Apparently there was a man who came to the island in 1837, just after the murder, and when the subject was brought up in conversation, 'he always made an evasive reply, such as I never meddle with other people's business'. Although the suspect (never named) was a modeller and a plasterer, as noted on the reward poster's description of the killer, and had drunk in the King's Arms, it was confirmed that he was on the island at the time of the murder.

The final episode in this mystery occurred in 1848, when one Charles Holland came under suspicion. He lived in Southampton and was employed by a cabinet maker. He wore dark clothing, lived near to the pub and was unemployed at the time of the crime. But, apart from resembling, in some respects, the description of the killer, there was nothing else against him and so he was not charged with the murder.

There was a long-standing belief that the case was one of suicide, though this was impossible because Eliza would have had to be left handed to have inflicted the wound that had killed her, and she was not. Furthermore, as *The Annual Register* of 1837 observed:

> *The insufficiency of motive for the murder has been urged as an argument for the probability of suicide, but who can pretend to judge of motives who remembers the case of Phynwick Williams, the woman stabber [also known as the Monster, a man who stabbed women in London in 1789–1790], and the many other 'monsters' who have from time to time, have appeared and wounded women indiscriminately, causelessly and without knowledge of, or provocation from them?*

We will never know who killed the unfortunate Eliza. Unlike some of the victims in this book, it is easy to feel a great deal of sympathy for her – young and with an unsullied character. She was probably killed for a very trivial reason – probably by a customer of the pub who had a grievance, real or imagined, against her. But who this could have been and why he took so violently against her is unknown. She probably had no inkling she was in mortal danger, for it would appear that after the customer came in, she served him, he paid and then, after drinking half of his pint, seized a knife and cut her throat, before dashing outside and into oblivion forevermore.

CHAPTER 3

Murder in Lambeth
1838

I tell you candidly I am the murderer
of Eliza Grimwood, and will put
myself in the hands of justice as soon
as possible.

On 28 May 1838, an inquest was held at the York Hotel on Waterloo Road on the body of one Eliza Grimwood, aged twenty-eight, who had a very different character from that of Eliza Davis, whose demise has just been chronicled. Yet their fates were exactly the same.

Eliza lived with George Hubbard, a bricklayer, who was married, but not to Eliza. Hubbard lived apart from his own wife. Eliza had, as the surgeon explained at the inquest, been horribly injured in a number of places. She had been stabbed in the abdomen and under the left breast with a sharp pointed instrument about half an inch wide. However, the wound which proved fatal was that in the neck, which extended almost from ear to ear and severed the windpipe. There was also a wound on her left thumb, probably caused when the woman tried to defend herself.

It was coyly said that Eliza 'was in the habit of taking persons home with her from theatres'. This probably means that she was a prostitute. Perhaps she and Hubbard lived off her earnings and he was quite happy with this arrangement, tactfully sleeping in another room when she was 'working'. On the Friday night before her death (25 May), she was at the Strand Theatre with a man 'who had the look of a foreigner – tall, pale, with large whiskers, and wore the garb of a gentleman'. They entered a cab together at the end of the performance and arrived at her home at about midnight. Neither was seen again.

As said, Hubbard and Eliza did not always share a bedroom. She often used a room on the ground floor, he on the first floor. On the following morning, he was going to work, but he noticed that Eliza's bedroom door was partly open. Investigating, he saw her partially undressed body on the floor, steeped in blood. He alerted the house's

The Strand Theatre. Eliza Grimwood and her client left here to go to her room. John Coulter's collection

other residents – a commercial traveller and the woman he lived with. Neither they nor the servant who slept on the ground floor heard anything during the night. But this was probably because, by the nature of the fatal wound, death would have been instantaneous.

Robbery may have been the motive. Eliza had had a purse with 10 or 11 sovereigns in it. This was missing. She also had a gold watch and £20 in a savings account. Initial suspicion fell on Hubbard. His razor was missing, as was one of his shirts. However, the nature of the wounds indicated that a weapon such as a razor could not have been used. Another possible clue was a rusty penknife which was discovered under the floorboards in a room in the house, but again this was dismissed as not being the weapon used, as it was too small. Waterloo Bridge and the roofs of neighbouring houses were examined in order to find the weapon, but these attempts were unsuccessful. A pair of kid gloves was also found at the scene of the crime.

Yet suspicions of Hubbard remained. Harriet Chaplin, Eliza's niece, said that Hubbard told her 'he would not mind shooting her, and that she had himself seen him strike her when angry'. On the other hand, Maria Glover, who lived in the same house as Eliza and Hubbard, said that the former 'never complained of ill-usage from Hubbard'. John Owen, a cooper of Cottage Place, Waterloo Road, probably saw the murderer on the early morning of Saturday, 26 May.

He saw a man wearing light drawers, and his shirt sleeves were tucked up to the elbows, and there was blood on his hands. He said 'Oh, Oh! I've done the deed; now how must I escape from it?' When, he was asked to identify the man he saw outside the house where Hubbard lived, he did not point to Hubbard. Owen, though, was not seen as a creditworthy witness.

Relations between Hubbard and Eliza were certainly volatile. Edmond Champneys, the constable of Epping, sent the London police information about Hubbard's activities in the previous summer. He had been staying in a cottage there and had paid court to a young woman, pretending to be single. Eliza appeared, and trouble flared up between them. Champneys wrote:

> *Eliza Grimwood came down and claimed him as her husband. She turned his box out of the cottage and some blows were given by Eliza which made his face bleed. Other persons saw them quarrelling in the Forest and saw Hubbard offer to strike Eliza . . . More quarrelling took place between them at a public house in Epping.*

Champneys also discovered Hubbard's missing shirt at the cottage he had stayed at in Epping.

Yet the killer might not have been Hubbard. Catherine Edwin had met Eliza at the theatre and saw her with a man. She said that Eliza had seen him on previous occasions. According to her:

> *He was an Italian, but could speak English fluently; and had been acquainted with the deceased for months. He was in the habit of going to see her. He appeared to be nearly six feet in height. The deceased had said to witness, on seeing him, 'Here comes my tormentor'.*

She had often seen the two together in the street. Once, when the three were together in a private room of a confectioners in Piccadilly, he asked Eliza to marry him. Eliza refused to answer. When the man threw off his cloak, something dropped to the ground. Catherine picked it up. It was a clasp knife. Drawing down a spring, the blade flew open, which was the width of a thumb nail. This may have been the murder weapon, especially because the cuts on Eliza's body would appear to have been made by such a knife.

The police followed up the matter, by going with Catherine to the shop in question. It was of no use. Charlotte Rosedale, who kept the shop, remembered that the two women had gone into the back room, but she had not overheard anything.

Catherine knew a little more about her friend's lover. She said that Eliza had referred to him as being 'a man of depraved habits'. He frequented the neighbourhood of the Spread Eagle pub in Regent Circus. He wore a ring which Eliza had given him. The words

Piccadilly Circus, c.1830s. Author's collection

'Semper Fidelis' were inscribed upon it. When Eliza refused to marry him, he threatened to throw her over the bridge. Eliza did not think he was a gentleman. Yet Maria Glover, who claimed to know Eliza better than anyone, said that she had never heard of the Italian nor the offer of marriage.

Inspector Arthur Field investigated Hubbard's antecedents and this enquiry had mixed results. Apparently Hubbard had 'hated his wife with a great deal of ill usage when she lived with him'. When Hubbard visited his mother in Mile End, the latter's house was searched and nothing relevant was found.

Despite there being little evidence against Hubbard, he was arrested and committed to Horsemonger Lane Prison. This was because a letter, allegedly by one John Walter Cavendish, had been received by the police, having being first addressed to the coroner, accusing Hubbard of the murder. The writer said he was the man who was with Eliza at the theatre and that, after they returned to Eliza's room, Hubbard had come down in a rage and ordered him from the premises. After a scuffle, the man left, leaving Eliza to Hubbard's attentions. He had changed his appearance so he would not be recognized and said he was an Englishman, not an Italian. He also said that Catherine's story was merely invented. The police tried to trace the writer, who they thought was one Mr Douglas McMillan, a stationer of Highgate. He had allegedly sent it via the Highgate post office.

Although he did admit visiting the post office with a letter on the same day that this one had been sent, he denied having sent it and the allegation was seen as a fabrication, especially as the writing and his own were dissimilar. Susan Humphries, the postmistress, was also uncertain whether McMillan had posted it. Had the writer been identified and had come forward to testify in person, the evidence would have been seen as important, but as its provenance was doubtful, it was dismissed.

There were other hoax letters from men pretending to be the killer. One was allegedly by Philip Jardine of Hornsey who wrote 'I tell you candidly I am the murderer of Eliza Grimwood, and will put myself in the hands of justice as soon as possible.' Another letter threatened one of the lawyers working on the case, reading, 'Indeed, you are a fine subject for the worms. Take care of your precious throat! The stiletto is yet further capable, and your person pretty well known.' The writer of this one stated that he was a Frenchman, as did another who claimed to be the murderer, who was struck by conscience but dared not confess to the authorities.

The mystery of the kid gloves also seemed to be cleared up. A Mr Skinner bought them from a glover on the Strand. He visited Harriet Chaplin in January and thought he may have left them there. She thought that Eliza, who had visited her, might have taken them, or Rebecca Ryan, a friend of Eliza's who accompanied her on that

Epping Forest, c.1910. George Hubbard and Eliza Grimwood quarrelled here.
Author's collection

occasion, may have removed them. Skinner said that he was not the man who accompanied Eliza home on that fatal night.

Hubbard was released after a week in gaol because there was no evidence against him. However, many people thought he was guilty and he had to be released in secret in case he was attacked by the mob. He later emigrated to America. An Italian was arrested because he resembled the man seen with Eliza, but was discharged. A reward of £50 for anyone who could identify the killer was offered by Lambeth parish, but it had no effect. Unless the killer had an accomplice who was willing to betray his friend, it could not be effectual, and this case was the work of a single killer.

The murder aroused much morbid curiosity. Crowds flocked to see the premises soon after the murder was known about. Eliza's possessions were sold on 13 June, to a packed audience. People were eager to see the bloodstained floor and see the belongings of the murdered woman. Her goods sold for £80. As *The Annual Register* noted, 'this, if true, would seem to prove, that the extraordinary appetite for the marvellous and the horrible displayed on this and similar occasions is not altogether confined to the lowest and most ignorant class of society in this country'.

Despite all the hard work put in by Field and his colleagues, they were unable to uncover the identity of the killer. Operations were scaled down after a few weeks of fruitless hard slog.

Interest in this unsolved murder continued in the following years. In March 1839, one George Berry, who claimed to be the son of William IV and that he had been tortured by the elderly Lord Melbourne, then Prime Minister, asserted that he had dramatic new evidence. He 'stated that Lord Melbourne was the person who murdered Eliza Grimwood in the Waterloo Road, which fact he could prove by undeniable evidence'. He had written to the Queen and to the sheriffs of Middlesex. Berry was deemed to be insane. In the following month he committed suicide by drowning in the Thames. Conspiracy theorists could have a field day exploring this angle. Yet the man seen leaving the house does not seem very much like the aristocratic premier.

A less dramatic revelation took place a few months later. A letter, allegedly by a Mr Duke of Chancery Lane, declared that the author 'will unravel that mystery on being assured of secrecy. I shall not be easy until I have betrayed the villain'. When Mr Duke, a law student, was questioned by the police, he denied that the letter was written by him and said that the handwriting bore no resemblance to his own.

Seven years after the murder, on 21 August 1845, one Private George Hill of the 67th Regiment of Infantry, stationed in Ireland, confessed to the crime before magistrates in Dublin. Field investigated the claim. He discovered that Hill was 'much addicted to drinking, and spending his time in the company of loose women'. Hill had been a petty criminal, stealing from his employers when working as a ticket collector on the London and Westminster Steam Boat Company, and had spent six months in prison for stealing a watch in Manchester. Despite having a wife and three children in Islington, he enlisted in the army in 1842, but his record noted he had deserted twice and been absent without permission once. Although he had lived near Waterloo Road in 1838, there seemed nothing to connect him to the murder.

Eventually, the real reason why he confessed was revealed. He said:

No, that I had made that statement under the influence of liquor and that he [I] had committed other acts of misconduct for the purpose of getting transported, as he [I] had a wish to leave the regiment in consequence of this tyrannical treatment.

Eliza's killer was never found. He was presumably the mysterious man who accompanied her back to her room and was seen later by Owen. Did he kill her for her money – 10 or 11 sovereigns – or was it a crime of passion? But whoever he was, he escaped, known to no one. There are other cases in this book with similar features – especially that of Harriet Buswell in 1872.

CHAPTER 4

Time is Called on the Clockmaker
1839

I feel certain that the robbery must have been committed by some persons who had a knowledge of the watch trade and were acquainted with the premises.

There was great alarm in the vicinity of Prince Street, Soho, on the night of Monday 3 June 1839. Loud screams of 'Fire' were heard and smoke billowed out of Robert Westwood's house. Yet there was even greater concern when Westwood's corpse was found. However, he had not died from fire or smoke. He had been murdered.

Westwood was aged about fifty-five at the time of his death and was a watch and clockmaker. He had been in the business for nearly three decades and was watchmaker to His Royal Highness, the Duke of Sussex. His household consisted of Mary, his wife, who was two decades his senior, Maria Petty, a servant, and Mr Gerard, a Frenchman who had lodged with them for ten years. Until recently Mr and Mrs Stephenson had lodged with them. While Mr Stephenson, a cabinet maker, had got on well with Westwood, they had been told to leave because of Mrs Stephenson's immorality – she often invited men back to her room, and may have been a prostitute. She was also violent and scratched her husband's face when he told her that they must find new lodgings.

Westwood's house had been burgled in 1822. Three men had effected an entry, tied him up and looted the premises. Over £800 worth of goods and money was stolen. However, one of the burglars, William Reading, a youth of seventeen or eighteen years, was tried for the crime, as was Benjamin Solomons, a Jew. The former was found guilty and was hanged. Since then, Westwood had taken to sleeping in a room downstairs, at the back of the shop, in order to safeguard its contents the better, though his wife slept upstairs.

Prince Street, Soho, 2006. Robert Westwood was murdered in a house here. Author's collection

Monday evening began conventionally. Westwood had left the premises at 5.30 pm and returned at 8.00 pm. Mrs Westwood went to bed at 11.00 pm, whilst her husband sat up and read. Gerard returned home about this time and was admitted by Maria Petty, the servant, who then locked the door behind him. At about 12.30 pm, Mrs Westwood began to hear noises from downstairs. It appeared as if there was a scuffle of some type, but she initially dismissed it as her husband letting the cat out. But she changed her mind when she heard groans. She became even more alarmed when she heard the main door being slammed. Finding Mr Gerard was asleep, she asked Maria to investigate.

The girl went downstairs and on entering the parlour, was almost suffocated by dense smoke. She went out into the street – the door was unlocked – and, being unable to shout 'Fire', asked a passerby to do so, which he did. Fire engines were quickly on the spot – the first being the parish fire engine. The flames were extinguished and then the partially burnt, but fully clothed, body of Westwood was found on the bed in the parlour.

Mr Smith, a surgeon in Dean Street, had been summoned. He pronounced life extinct, caused by a number of dreadful wounds. The first of these was a blow to the right temple, just above the eye, caused by some heavy, blunt instrument. Then there was a terrible gash on the left side of the throat and extending most of the way around the neck, severing the major arteries. Finally there was another slash to the neck. Clearly these had been inflicted by a different weapon, a very sharp one.

Superintendent Baker and Inspector Jervis investigated the murder. They searched the room for the weapon, and eventually found a heavy iron window weight in the passage leading to the street door. It was about five or six pounds in weight and twelve to fourteen inches long. A few hairs were found adhering to the weight. This was certainly one of the weapons used, dropped by the killer as he fled from the house. The other weapon was a white-handled paper knife, which was found in the drawer of a sideboard in the parlour and its blade was stained with much blood, although it had been hastily wiped.

Was robbery the motive? After checking the stock book, it was ascertained that about sixty of the most valuable watches had been stolen. Each was worth between 10 and 40 guineas. In all, about £2,000 worth of stock was missing. Money boxes had also been opened – they had contained sovereigns and silver. The killer probably had a good idea of where the money and valuables were held.

The inquest was held on the following day at the Plough in Rupert Street. After the jury had seen the corpse, Smith recounted the medical evidence. He noted that the side of the head had been battered and the skull was fractured in several places. He added that it could not be known whether there were any injuries on the hands as they were too badly burnt.

Maria told the court that Westwood employed a journeyman watchmaker, one Alfred Bannister. He worked in the room above the back kitchen in the daytime, but had left the premises by about 8.00 pm. She added that she had left the house to have her supper beer, returning at about 9.00 pm. The inquest was then adjourned to the following day.

The doctors could not determine exactly which wound killed Westwood. They thought that he had been pulled onto the bed before the fire had been started. Mr French, a surgeon, thought that Westwood might have been stunned first, and then killed by another blow shortly afterwards.

PC Thomas Chilman had been the first policeman on the scene, and was called upon to give his evidence. He had found Maria with two men. These were George Robinson and Robert Peake (ironically one Robert Peake was a witness to Westwood's will, made in 1825). Robinson had entered the house after he had heard the alarm. He had a wound in his cheek, which he said was a burn, despite a surgeon contradicting him. When he was inside, he put down his hat and took Westwood's instead of his own.

Mrs Westwood had to be carried into the room on a chair. When asked if she suspected anyone, she said that Mrs Stephenson, who was 'of a most venomous, spiteful disposition', might be an object of suspicion. She thought Mrs Stephenson had not returned her house key. She also said that she believed her husband had received threatening anonymous letters two years previously, but she had not seen them. A police inspector said that the fire had probably been caused by a candle being lit under the bed.

Frederick Owen told the court he had seen two men in their early thirties by the entrance to Westwood's house. He did not think they looked respectable, but nor did he recall that they were carrying anything heavy. One of these men was the aforementioned Robinson; the other was presumably Peake.

Westwood's employees gave evidence. Bannister said that his employer had left the house at between 5.00 and 6.00, returning at 7.50 pm. He last saw his master when the latter closed his shop, as usual, at 9.00 pm. He said that he had never heard Mrs Stephenson threaten Westwood. Relations between Charles Le Roche, the foreman, and Westwood were not good. Bannister said the two had argued because Le Roche had been late to work recently, but he had not been at Westwood's as far as he knew, on the day of the murder. Le Roche had no idea who could have committed the crime. But he did say that it would be relatively easy to smuggle the stolen goods out of the country for sale. He said, 'I feel certain that the robbery must have been committed by some persons who had a knowledge of the watch trade and were acquainted with the premises'. Oddly enough, he was not asked about his quarrel with Westwood. Gerard, the lodger, was questioned but had little to say, as he was asleep at the time, and had no suspicions against anyone.

Finally the Stephensons gave their evidence. The couple were now separated. Mr Stephenson had seen Westwood six days before the murder, as he had to settle his accounts with him. He had told him that his wife still had their key to his house. He also said that his wife was suicidal and that her good name had been defamed. Mrs Stephenson then spoke. She claimed that she had forgotten about the key and had lent it to no one. She also said that the people who visited her were members of her family.

The jury reached the only verdict they could – murder by person or persons unknown. The coroner was asked to apply to the government to increase the reward money for Westwood's killer. A reward of £100 had already been set. It was soon raised to £200 and finally to £400.

The contents of Westwood's will, which was drawn up in the decade before his death, do not help. All his property was to go to his wife and there seems nothing to implicate her in his murder.

There were numerous men against whom suspicion was directed. The first was William Campion, who had worked for Westwood for three years, until 1835. According to Inspector Pearce, he was 'known to be a bad character in the trade and can get no employment'. With his contacts in Paris and Holland, it was thought that, if he were the killer, he would be able to sell the watches abroad easily enough. On 22 June Pearce found him and remarked 'he was perfectly easy to answer my questions'. Campion was working for one George Harrison, a watchmaker near Pentonville. His lodgings in Wellington Street were searched – to no effect. His landlady said he was never out of the house after 11.00 at night, and that 'their [sic] could not be a more regular man', though he did spend most of his money on drink. Harrison said that Campion was at work until 10.00 on the night of the murder and at work the following day at 7.00 am. Pearce concluded, 'it is my opinion from general observation and the inquiry I have made that there is not the slightest suspicion attached to him'.

Another suspect was Nicholas Williams Carron. He was a glazier and paper hanger and lived only two doors away from Westwood. Two days after the murder he left home, 'in a very exalted state', and went to Liverpool, there taking a steam ship to New York. He was said to be 'of dissolute habits and known to be in embarrassing circumstances previous to his absconding'. He knew the Westwood premises well, having done some work there, and had a sash weight, such as the one which killed Westwood and often carried one with him. However, it seems more probable that Carron, who was in desperate financial straits and was being pressed by creditors, took this chance to begin a new life.

Thirdly, a strange man stole a boat at Broadstairs and was next found at Boulogne. He was a German by the name 'John Sunens'. However, there was no known link with him and the murder; only the coincidence that he had fled the country just after it had occurred.

Could the motive have been personal antagonism? Westwood was said to be 'a gentleman of extremely irritable temper'. A couple of years before, a disgruntled customer came to see him to return a watch which was not working. Westwood snatched the watch from the man and flung it to the floor before destroying it. Westwood was summoned before the magistrates for assault and had to reimburse the man. On another occasion, Westwood had threatened an unhappy customer with a pistol. Again he was fined. As has been noted, he had had arguments with Le Roche and had caused the Stephensons to be thrown out of the house. He must have been a difficult man to live and work with, as well as being aggressive towards strangers.

Pearce certainly thought the murder was the work of a gang. He believed the criminals were 'connected with those tried and convicted of a previous burglary of the house of the unfortunate gentleman, it being evident among other circumstances that a considerable degree of malice was used in mangling the body of their victim'. The gang consisted of the following men. The first was George Redgrave, who once lived in Clerkenwell and began to wear new clothes instead of his old shabby ones just after the murder. He was a friend of the late William Reading. Could Westwood's murder be revenge for the hanging of the youth for the burglary of 1822? Samuel Cotterell was another Clerkenwell burglar and likewise vanished shortly after the murder. James Harding was another gang member, and landlord of the Hare on Cambridge Heath. He had recently gone to Brighton. Finally there was Reading's brother, a watchmaker of Mile End. Pearce concluded 'My belief is that they are the parties concerned, whether or not anything will transpire to lead to their detection'. Yet there seems to have been no subsequent investigation of these men.

Finally, in September 1843, Henry Stocker, a prisoner in Newgate, claimed the killer was one Laver or Lever, who had stunned Westwood and then cut his throat. The motive was revenge and the man was still in the country. However, on close investigation, it was found that 'the whole statement is a fabrication on the part of Stocker'.

It is probable that robbery was, at least in part, the motive. Anyone killing for hatred or revenge would probably not have risked discovery whilst they stole from their victim. The question is: how did they get into the house? The door was locked. Did Westwood let his killer in himself? Or did the thief pick the lock or possess a key himself? It seems certain that, however the killer entered the house, he quickly and quietly disposed of Westwood, helped himself to his possessions and then left the house, slamming the door as he did so. By the time the alarm was raised, he had made his escape. And nothing more was ever heard of him.

CHAPTER 5

Method and Murderer Unknown
1850

I feel, therefore, unable to account for the death of the deceased. If I was obliged to give an opinion, she might have died from fright.

I t is rare for the method of death to be as mysterious as the identity of the murderer. Usually, the cause of death is all too obvious – and bloody. Yet this is a case in which both were equally baffling to investigators.

Mr John Maddle (1781–1863) had been a successful shopkeeper and, aged sixty-nine in 1850, was a widower of independent means. At the time of his death in the following decade his assets were worth somewhat under £2,000. He lived at Claremont Place, Wandsworth Road, with his housekeeper, Sarah Snelling, who had been in his employ since at least 1841. On the morning of Sunday, 28 April 1850, he left home to attend the service held at St Paul's, Clapham Parish Church. It was a few minutes before 11.00 am. He returned home just after 1.00 pm and, as usual, rang the bell at the gate for admittance. All perfectly normal.

It was from that moment on that events took an unusual turn. No one answered the bell. He rang it several times, but with the same lack of response. Maddle then tried the garden gate, which was, unusually, unfastened. He entered the house by the washroom and went into the kitchen. It was then that he saw the body of his housekeeper, lying on her back, with her legs stretching over the threshold of the kitchen door and her head near the French windows. After feeling the body and concluding life was extinct, Maddle roused his neighbours.

Two eventually arrived: Mrs Staples and Mrs Travash. According to *The Times*, they:

> ... *found the deceased lying as stated, but under most extraordinary circumstances. Her right leg was partly drawn up under the body, and*

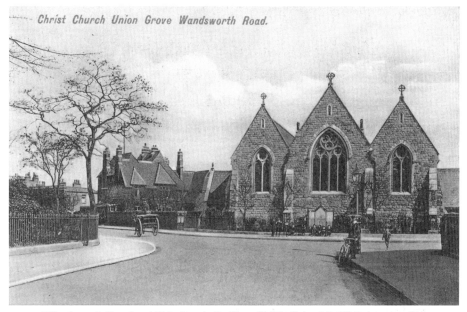

Wandsworth Road, c.1900. Sarah Snelling died in John Maddle's house, which was on this road. Author's collection

entangling the foot, which was without a shoe (which was missing), was a coil of rope hanging out clothes; her head rested on six or seven folds of carpeting. And within six inches of the head was a basin containing about a pint of clean water. The face, hands and other parts of the body were cold. There was not the smallest contortion of features nor, so far as was observed, any marks of personal violence. The eyes were closed as if in sleep, and but for the ghastly expression of the face it could have hardly been imagined but she slept.

John Parrott, the police surgeon, who arrived just after 2.00 pm, could find no marks of violence, and his father, also a doctor, agreed, and they thought the deceased had been in good health.

Inspector Coleman investigated and found that the house had been ransacked by very inexpert thieves. Every drawer, box and chest had been opened and its contents emptied, and a screwdriver from the tool box in the house had been used to force them. Maddle thought that a gold watch, some jewellery and plate was missing. Yet there was no sign that an entry into the house had been forced. Suspicious-looking men were seen near the house at about noon. One was short, with a blotched face and a dark coat and carrying a bundle. His companion was tall and thin, with curly hair and wore a dark coat. And there was another man. They were going towards Balham.

On the following day, the inquest was held at the Nag's Head on the Wandsworth Road. The jury had to view the corpse, which lay in the kitchen. They then heard Parrott giving the medical evidence. He had not found any blood, and said that the clothes had been undisturbed. He then had the corpse stripped, but had been unable to find any obvious cause of death. There was no smell of poison and the organs were healthy. However, he did find marks of a recent inflammation of the stomach and two teaspoons of indigested matter therein.

Maddle was the next to give evidence about the deceased. He said that she was thirty-three years old (but she must almost certainly have been older), had been with him for twelve years and had proved reliable and sober, but added that her constitution was not strong. He employed her 'because she was old and ugly, that he might not be tempted by her'. He recalled her letting him out of the house at 10.35 am and said she seemed cheerful. He assumed she then locked the door as usual. He had asked her to prepare dinner. He thought that someone must have moved her to the position in which she was found, as there was no evidence that this work had been begun when he returned. Maddle added that there had been an attempted burglary two months previously.

The inquest was then adjourned for a week in order that an analysis of the intestines be carried out. However, there was some disagreement on this matter. Mr Higgs, the coroner, refused to allow Parrott to apply to Professor Taylor or Dr Letheby to analyse the contents of the stomach. Parrott then asked the Police Commissioner, but was told that funds did not permit such expenditure. Higgs was asked again, but refused. The Police Commissioner then referred the matter to the Home Secretary for a decision.

Meanwhile, the police made attempts to find the burglars. Apparently on the evening before the crime, a tall thin man, in a black coat, had asked one Dr Hales of Blackfriars' Road, for 6 pence worth of chloroform. The man said he needed it to make a woman unconscious while he removed one of her teeth. Hales refused and the man continued to ask him, but had to join his companions in the street empty-handed. Hales thought that these men were the ones who had been seen near Maddle's house on the following day.

If the motive was burglary, the haul was very limited. A gold watch, two or three rings and about £3–£4 had been stolen. Maddle was vague about what had been taken and exaggerated the extent of the thefts. Some items allegedly missing were found on the premises. Suspicion fell on him. Maddle himself was accused by his late housekeeper's nephews of being responsible for her death. The police thought so, too, and Superintendent Thomas Bicknell wrote in his report:

The mystery attached to this case and the apparent equivocation of Mr Maddle have induced the police to watch him carefully, and they find him all through, to exhibit a disposition to violent temper, a perversion of truth, an artfulness of manner and evident symptoms of avariciousness.

This impression was strengthened when Inspector Coleman heard Maddle say, at Sarah's funeral, 'Ah, poor girl, she is gone, she will tell no tales'. Yet Maddle had left the house at 10.40 am and one witness noted that Maddle arrived at church at about 11.00 am, so he seems to be ruled out as he had a strong alibi. He may have been an unpleasant character, but he does not appear to have been a killer.

Mr Venables, another witness, came forward. He recalled Maddle telling him on the Sunday, 'There is my poor girl lying dead; have you heard any noise?' Venables had neither heard nor seen anything suspicious, but said that someone could have got into the house without him seeing anyone.

The inquest reopened on 7 May. Parrott explained that he had analysed the contents of the stomach for poisons such as arsenic, prussic acid and oxalic acid. There was no trace of chloroform either. He declared:

I feel, therefore, unable to account for the death of the deceased. If I was obliged to give an opinion, she might have died from fright. Instances have occurred when nothing abnormal presented themselves. A fright might produce a fateful syncope.

Another witness, Mrs Jane Stevenson, said that the deceased 'appeared a feeble person'. Similarly, Sarah's daughter declared that her mother was 'in weak health and affected with shortness of breath'.

Sarah must have died before 12.45 because James Clarke from the Nag's Head had come to the house to deliver beer. He had knocked three times and there was no response. She probably died much earlier as there was no indication that she had begun to prepare Maddle's lunch.

The inquest ended inconclusively; although it was clear that Sarah had been murdered, how this had happened was still a mystery. A few days later, two men, Henry Stark and William Knight, were apprehended as being concerned in a number of burglaries, including that at Maddle's house. Knight, when arrested, was found to have a number of housebreaking implements in his possession. He was found guilty before a magistrate of having the intent to commit burglary and was sentenced to three months. His companion was released.

No one, however, was ever charged with causing the death of Sarah Snelling. It is possible that burglars broke into the house not long after

Clapham Parish Church, c.1900. John Maddle was worshipping here when Susan died. Author's collection

Maddle had left. They may have been watching it and so chose the easiest time at which to effect an entry. It is certainly probable that Sarah died of shock. Witnesses had testified to her weak health and the entry of unknown men intent on burglary would certainly have had a shocking effect which may have led to her death. This seems most possible. But as to who they were, we are no wiser than the police at the time. Perhaps Knight and Stark were responsible, but there was no evidence to prove that they had done it. In any case, it seems likely that they, or whoever broke in, did not intend that she should have died. Certainly the act of placing towels under the dead woman's head suggests that some respect was paid to her.

Or could it have been an accident? Mrs Dennis of Wandsworth Road said that Sarah had a regular visitor, an elderly man who often came to see her and was admitted by her. Apparently,

She used to smile and receive him with apparent pleasure. I have known him to stop frequently two hours or more ... He was of shabby appearance in dark clothes ... five feet six inches height, middle size, carried his head down and walked slow.

Could Sarah have died during a visit from this man, who was probably a friend, who then fled? Perhaps he faked the burglary in order to throw suspicion on another quarter? This would make her death an accident, not murder, and would account for the lack of any cause of death.

CHAPTER 6

Kidnap and Murder
1853

... one of the most barbarous and horrible – one of the most cruel and deliberate murders that had ever been committed.

As we shall see, children were occasionally kidnapped and murdered in this period and this book records a number of these cases. It was on 19 December 1853 that the naked corpse of a lad was found by a man called Simpson, who worked for one Mr Clarke at Hammersmith, in a ditch by the pathway between Friar's Place and East Acton. He had probably lain there for about a day. The body was identified as being that of the thirteen-year-old Richard Medhurst. He had worked for Mr Thirtwell, a hairdresser in Old Street, and lived in Clerkenwell with his father. An hour after the corpse had been found, it was seen by police sergeant Earthy, who described it as 'a fearful spectacle – the right eye was black partially down the cheek, and the bones were almost protruding through the skin'. He also saw marks on the wrists and ankles, probably made by cords. Shortly after the discovery, the lad's grandfather died, his death being doubtless accelerated by the news of his grandson's untimely demise.

A reward of £100 was offered by the government to anyone who could give information about the killer and about whoever deposited the body where it was found. The police in all the metropolitan divisions were asked for assistance, though most could only send negative replies. It was known that Medhurst had disappeared on 31 October 1853 from outside a coffee house in Old Street, St Luke's, and had been driven away in a chaise cart in the direction of Shoreditch. The man driving the cart was described thus, 'About thirty-five years old, five foot eight inches high, dark hair and whiskers, dressed in a dark overcoat, light coat underneath, and corduroy trousers'. Medhurst was also described: 'of small stature, and dressed when last seen in a tweed coat with velvet collar, blue plaid trousers, red and green plaid neckerchief, blue cloth cap with braid on the top, and lace boots'.

There was a great deal of speculation as to what had happened. One theory was that there was 'in or near to the metropolis a gang of ruffians, banded together for the purpose of decoying young persons from their homes for some vile purpose, and afterwards making away with their victims'. Several other young persons had been missing in London at this time, too. A gentleman resident in Hammersmith had recently sent a female servant out of the house on an errand and she had been attacked by a man who tried to drag her away into a cart. Fortunately her resistance proved successful and other people arrived on the scene, though her assailant drove away. The police thought that this attack might have been the work of the same men who carried Medhurst away.

The inquest took place at the Goldsmith's Arms in East Acton on 20 and 26 January 1854. Much of the inquest was taken up with the medical evidence which showed how the boy met his death. Dr Robert Glover of the Royal Free Hospital was the principal witness. He had examined the lad's stomach and made a chemical analysis as well as inspecting it microscopically. He said, 'I found nothing except the ordinary particles of mucus, with some globules which denoted inflammation. The mucus surface of the stomach was highly inflamed, and there were six or seven spots of echymose blood.'

The coroner asked how might such effects be reached. Glover suggested that they might be the result of starvation, cold, or an

The Goldsmith's Arms (left), East Acton, c.1900. The inquest on Richard Medhurst was held here. Author's collection

THE VILLAGE, EAST ACTON.

irritant poison, but that he had found no evidence of the latter. When pressed, he thought that the cause of death was the combination of starvation and external violence. There was certainly much to show that the boy had been deprived of food. This was due to the fact that the lungs were severely inflamed and cut to pieces. The other organs were examined for traces of poison but none was found. Glover concluded:

> *I have no doubt that before the boy died he was reduced to a great state of debility; and in that weak state to which he was reduced, very little violence would cause his death, and there were marks of violent external injury, particularly on the nose and eye, which were the results of certainly more than one severe blow.*

Mr Thomas Francis, a surgeon resident in East Acton, then came forward. He had previously thought that tubercular disease might have been the cause of death. He tended to agree with Glover that the boy had been reduced to a great state of weakness before the blows which had killed him were struck, but he would not like to state categorically that these blows had been fatal.

Apart from the medical evidence, Inspector Beckerson was able to announce more startling news. Richard Watkins, a chaise maker of Enfield, told the police that he had made a chaise of the type described for one George Wildbore, a publican of the George Inn at Bishop's Stortford in Hertfordshire (he also owned the New Inn in Waltham Cross). This man had since been apprehended on suspicion. Furthermore, George Jackson, a thirteen year old of Allen Street, Clerkenwell, had identified Wildbore as the man who drove Medhurst away in his cart. The coroner, however, was wary of such an identification, arguing that a number of similarly dressed men should be shown in the company of the suspect, in order that they be picked out by the witness. Detective Inspector Thornton protested that Jackson had been sent to a number of public houses in Bishop's Stortford before making the correct identification. However, another lad, Lee, who had also seen the kidnapper, had been shown Wildbore in the company of six plain clothed policemen and had been unable to select him.

What had happened was that Jackson had been with Medhurst at about 6.50 on 31 October 1853. They had been walking along Old Street, and a man approached them, asking if they would hold his horse for him. Jackson agreed, but he was pushed aside by Medhurst. Both of them followed the man until they came to a horse and cart, which were being held by another boy. The latter was given a penny and left.

The man in question was full faced, wore a broad brimmed hat, had shiny boots and trousers. Jackson was certain he would recognize the man if he saw him again. Medhurst then got into the cart and drove away with the stranger towards Shoreditch. It was a dark night.

After the discovery of Medhurst's body, Jackson had approached the police and told them his story. With the circulation of the wanted man's description, Wildbore came under suspicion. Sergeant Gunn accompanied Jackson to Bishop's Stortford. Gunn went to the George Inn and then called for Jackson to go there. Wildbore was in the parlour. In the presence of Jackson, Gunn addressed the publican,

There has been a boy named Medhurst taken away from Old Street in London, by a man with a horse and chaise. The body has since been found dead at East Acton, and this boy says 'you are the man who took him away'.

Wildbore looked hard at the boy, who stated 'Yes, you are the man'. Gunn then told Wildbore that they would search his premises in order to find a horse and chaise cart. Wildbore obliged and ordered a man to open the stables for inspection. Within the stables were a dog cart and a chaise cart. Jackson said that the dog cart was certainly similar to the one that Medhurst was taken away on. Yet nothing else suspicious could be found on the premises.

Wildbore protested his innocence. He said that he had not been to London for six months. Gunn said that he must accompany him to London, but not before the publican sent for his solicitor and then put his great coat on. Jackson then identified the coat as being the one the kidnapper wore. Wildbore was taken before the Clerkenwell Magistrates' Court and remanded in custody, despite a request by the solicitor for bail. It had been hoped that Wildbore could have been brought to the inquest, but he was before the magistrates on the same day so this was not possible.

Returning to the inquest, the coroner then began to sum up. He said that there was little doubt that this was a case of murder, 'one of the most barbarous and horrible – one of the most cruel and deliberate murders that had ever been committed'. The jury wished for an adjournment in order that more evidence might be made available, though they agreed that it was a case of murder.

Meanwhile, Wildbore was once again brought before the Clerkenwell Magistrates' Court. Jackson was found to be an unreliable witness. On seeing Sergeant Earthy in plain clothes, he identified him as the kidnapper. Mr Hawkins, on Wildbore's behalf, had produced a number of witnesses who could provide an alibi for his client. However, Wildbore had lied. He had in fact been to London on the day of the kidnap, but he had travelled down by railway and had returned to

Bridge Street, Bishop's Stortford

Bishop's Stortford, c.1900. The publican of the George, George Wildbore, was suspected of murder. Author's collection

Bishop's Stortford at 5.40 – half an hour before the kidnap is said to have taken place. He had then dined with Frederick Sewell, a vet, at Waltham Cross and then taken tea with his nieces and a nephew. Finally, he did not leave home until the following day.

Although Hawkins said that the police had done their duty, he was convinced that his client was innocent. The magistrates agreed with him and concluded that there was no real evidence against Wildbore. He was duly released, to the cheering of his friends. It seems very unlikely that he was the killer, as he was fifty-eight years old at the time of the kidnap/murder, and the man seen with Medhurst was only in his thirties.

There had been a sighting of Medhurst in a lodging house in King Street, Hammersmith, in the previous November. Mr Clarke, the owner, recalled that a lad had been there for two weeks, with a woman. The boy said he would return, but did not. The lad declared he was an orphan, but had an uncle. He had also stayed at the Coach and Horses in Hammersmith before he came to Mr Clarke's, but it seems uncertain whether this was Medhurst as he was not an orphan. Presumably, it is coincidence that the man who discovered the corpse was an employee of Mr Clarke?

Another possible clue was the fact that Wildbore was alleged to have an uncle, one Captain Henry Hemmesely who lived in Acton.

Yet the captain lived in Chapel House, Mattock Lane, Ealing (two and a half miles from East Acton), and the sixty-two year old was respectable and a well-known gentleman, serving as a poor law guardian. The police did not think this was relevant information.

But if Wildbore did not kidnap and then murder Medhurst, who did? There was no doubt that he had been kidnapped on 31 October, and then killed several weeks later. He had been starved of food and became so weak that blows to his body killed him in early December and then he had been dumped in the countryside a few miles from the capital at East Acton. Why had he been kidnapped? Not for any financial gain. Perhaps it was due to sadism or/and perverse sexual desires – or what would now be termed paedophilia. Despite the offer of a reward, no one was ever convicted of this most heinous crime.

CHAPTER 7

The Waterloo Bridge Murder 1857

... all has remained shrouded in mystery ... and the perpetrators have contrived to baffle the closest enquiries of the police ...

ccording to *The Annual Register* of 1857: '"Murder will out" is an adage that bears the approval of many generations, but its correctness, under all circumstances, may well be doubted, when the mysterious affair of this day is borne in mind. That a foul and deliberate murder had been committed there can be no doubt; for although the inferences which lead to this conclusion spring but from trifling incidents, still the reasoning which conduced to them is irresistible. But beyond the fact of a crime having been committed all has remained shrouded in mystery which at first flung over the matter, and the perpetrators have contrived to baffle the closet enquiries of the police, although at times there appeared some clue to their discovery.'

It all began in the grey mist of the early morning of 9 October 1857. Two youths, James Barber and Frank Kelsby, were rowing from the north side of the Thames to the opposite side, towards a barge which belonged to James's elder brother, at about 5.30 am. They noticed a bundle resting on one of the abutments of Waterloo Bridge and went to investigate. The bundle was actually a carpet-bag. It was locked and corded and much of the cord hung down into the water. Thinking they had found a prize indeed, they carried it off.

When they reached the barge, they showed it to James's brother. It was only when they opened it that they found the full horror of its contents, which were:

> ... *the mutilated fragments of a human body. Twenty pieces of what had recently been a living creature were exposed to view with every incident of horror. Limbs had been sawn into bits, flesh had been hacked from bones, the trunk had been disembowelled, and the head was wanting.*

Waterloo Bridge. Parts of a corpse of an unknown man were found near here. John Coulter's collection

The elder boy took the bag and its gruesome contents to Bow Street Police Station. It was here that the police examined them and a clearer picture emerged. Apart from the portions of the body, there was almost a complete set of clothes; coat, waistcoat, trousers, underwear, socks and shirt, but no shoes or hat. There was no mark on any of these clothes to indicate where it had been bought. Yet the make of clothing was foreign; the socks were said to be German. They had been pierced in various places, the inference being that the victim (a man) had been stabbed while still alive and wearing his clothes. The front parts of the clothing were saturated with blood. The weapon must have been a sharp pointed knife or dagger.

The clothes were of the highest quality. The sleeves of the overcoat were lined with red silk and it was made of the finest material. This indicated that whoever the deceased was, he had been fairly prosperous.

One initial theory was that the whole thing was 'a childish freak on the part of the students of a neighbouring hospital'. This theory was demolished at the inquest which was held soon afterwards. The body had not been chopped up for anatomical research.

Inspector MacKenzie summoned Mr Paynter, the police surgeon, from his practice in the Strand. Paynter investigated the remains on the same day and made his report at the inquest. He had previously fitted together the various bodily parts and found that they formed a complete corpse – almost. Crucially, the head, the hands and the feet were missing, as well as a few smaller bones. All the main bones had been sawn into at least two parts and all had pieces of tendon and muscle attached. Hardly any skin adhered to the bones. Short dark hairs were found, indicating that the body was that of an adult male in middle age. The remains had been preserved in brine for some time after death.

The victim had met his death by being stabbed in the chest. Paynter found a small wound between the ribs, where a weapon had been thrust and then removed. This was probably a sharp double-bladed dagger, such as a poniard. A number of thrusts had been made into the victim's body. He thought that a fine, narrow, saw had been used to chop up the body after death. He said that the saw had not been used until some time after death, because the body had become rigid, as noted from the stiffened limbs. The body had been taken out of the brine a few days before it had been deposited at Waterloo Bridge. Finally he noted that there were some fine, long hairs which must have belonged to a woman.

Henry Errington, toll keeper on Waterloo Bridge, and a former policeman, had additional evidence to reveal. He had been on duty at 11.30 pm on the night of 8 October. He said, 'I remember seeing a woman come up from the Strand side [i.e. the north bank of the Thames]. She was alone – and had a carpet-bag with her.' He was certain that this was the same bag which was now produced in court. She paid her halfpenny to cross the bridge and took her bag with her as she passed through the turnstile. She had some difficulty with this and Errington suggested she ask for help.

Errington helped her and lifted up the bag by the handles. He noted that it was mostly made of leather and had a bright flower as a pattern on the bag. He also noticed what the woman looked like. 'Her hair looked as if it had been powdered and plastered thickly down on her forehead ... She spoke rather gruff; it was certainly on a masculine tone of voice.' However, Errington denied that the person he saw could have been a short man when the idea was suggested to him. Her height might have been about five feet three inches. She was a short woman and 'rather stoutish'. Errington noted that she seemed in a hurry and thought she was trying to catch a train from Waterloo which left at 11.45 pm. He never saw her again.

It was presumed that she must have lowered the carpet bag into the Thames with rope attached to it, intending the current to take it out to sea. She was also carrying a large brown parcel. This was never found, but probably contained the head, feet and hands of the deceased, and was doubtless thrown off the bridge and carried out to sea by the tide.

The inquest was then adjourned for two weeks in order for the police to investigate the matter further and so that a more detailed medical report could be made.

The police made enquiries. They thought that it would have been difficult for the woman to have carried her weighty possessions any distance. Therefore they tried to discover if a hansom cab had taken her to the bridge and asked if anyone had seen anyone helping her with her burdens. Both avenues of enquiry drew a blank. Possibly the murder had taken place in a building near to the bridge, where it was noted there were a number of 'houses of ill-fame'. Experienced tailors were asked to examine the victim's clothes, but could only say they were made abroad. The public were also asked to examine them, but, again, without success. It was unlikely that scraps of clothing would have jogged anyone's memory anyway. A better policy would have been to try and recreate the clothing worn by the deceased, mount them on a tailor's dummy and exhibit it to the public in order that someone might remember having seen them. There were two possible further leads. These were a bag washed up in Lambeth and the discovery of human heads in Hyde Park. Yet the former proved to be a set of burglar's tools and the latter parts of bodies used for anatomy.

The police also offered a reward of £300 to anyone who could give information leading to the arrest and conviction of the killer(s). This amount was over a year's wage for many men, so was a tempting sum.

Another clue was contained in a letter from Mr Richards, the chief of the Stafford Police. He told how, on 29 September, one Hugh Patterson stayed at the house of Mr John Lea, a local shoe manufacturer. Patterson had recently arrived from Australia and was intending to travel to London to transact business, before returning to his native Scotland. He carried a large carpet bag, which, he claimed, contained £3,800 in gold. Patterson was aged between thirty and forty, had dark hair and was five feet seven inches in height. As with the murdered man, his coat sleeves had red linings. This promising lead does not seem to have been followed up.

When the jury was reassembled and the inquest continued, Dr Alfred Taylor fully agreed with Paynter's remarks, but added a number of further observations of his own. The remains were those of an adult male, at least five feet nine inches in height. He could find no physical peculiarities which could help identify the man, except that he was probably very hairy. There were no marks of disease or of violence inflicted during life, saving the stab wound which Paynter had identified as the cause of death. That wound probably penetrated the heart and caused almost instant death.

He also reiterated the point that the body had not been dissected in any skilful or medical manner. Someone quite ignorant of the subject had cut it up, as shown by the fact that organs had been severed and destroyed. This cutting had occurred between eighteen and twenty-four hours after death. The body had then been partly boiled and salted. He thought that the murder occurred in the last week of September, but could not pinpoint the time of death with any greater accuracy.

Further evidence was given by Samuel Ball, who corroborated that which Errington had previously given. He also noticed the face of the woman on the bridge and said, 'She had a sallow complexion and rather sunken eyes, with a mark on the left cheek, near the nose, which I took to be a mole. The hair was a kind of white, but it did not look a natural colour. I saw her features quite distinctly, but did not take any notice of her dress.' Ball also saw a tall man on the south side of the bridge, walking towards the opposite end of the bridge, but did not particularly notice him, nor could he identify him. This man was never identified.

The jury brought in the only possible verdict: that the remains were those of an adult man and he had been killed by person or persons unknown. Despite a number of people coming to see the remains to check whether they were those of a missing relative or friend, none could identify him. Despite a reward of £300 for the killer, no one ever came forward to claim it.

According to Major Arthur Griffiths, writing in 1899, 'The police had reason to believe that the man murdered was a Swedish sailor belonging to some ship then lying on the Thames'. But if this was the case, why did the police not search all ships on the Thames? Perhaps they did, but met with no positive results.

As with most murder cases, there was always someone willing to come forward and confess. In late December 1857, Thomas Pedlar, an army deserter who tried to hang himself at Colchester barracks, claimed that he knew the truth of the affair. He said that the victim was a farmer, not a foreigner. He said that he was one of several men who killed the man in London for the £60 he had on his possession. Yet when he was closely questioned by the police, 'he said it was all humbug, and he knew no more about the murder than he had read in the papers'. When brought before the magistrates, he retracted his earlier story. It was thought his mind was deranged and he was handed back to the military authorities.

Another rumour came to light in 1859. An elderly Irish woman called 'Biddy' sold fruit in London and believed she was dying. She called for a priest to make her last confession and was overheard by another woman. The latter claimed that Biddy said that she had been employed by two men to carry the bundle across the bridge. Nothing seems to have come of this.

Colchester Barracks, c.1900. A soldier at these barracks confessed to the murder.
Author's collection

It would seem that there were two people in the matter, at least; a man and a woman, though precisely what part each played is another question. Did the man kill the unknown man and was helped to dispose of the body by a female accomplice? Or vice versa? And who was the victim? Perhaps it was Hugh Patterson from Australia. There may have been very few people in Britain who could identify him, even though his name and rough description appeared in *The Times*. It seems odd that the inquest proceedings make no reference to him – did the Metropolitan Police not take up the leads offered by their Midlands colleagues? Presumably not. He does fit the description of the victim and, if he was carrying a large sum of gold, this alone supplies the motive. Might he have gone into a brothel or tavern and accidentally let slip he was carrying great wealth and so been the victim of an opportunist theft and murder?

His killer(s) must have feared that he might have been identified, hence the removal of head, feet and hands. Therefore, his relationship to them may have been known (perhaps he was seen in their company), and so they had to remove this incriminating link to themselves. It is also probable that the deed took place somewhere which would have incriminated the killer(s) – perhaps their house, flat, business address or an address they frequently haunted. Therefore the body had to be removed and dumped somewhere where it would be totally anonymous. So it had to be hacked into small enough pieces that it could be put into a bag and removed. Somewhere, a man had vanished into thin air, and no one put this and the grim discovery together. Had they done so, the guilty would have paid the price. The motive was probably money.

Another theory, for what it is worth, was mentioned by Sir Robert Anderson in his memoirs. He stated that in 1870 a French detective, identified as 'Maxwell', gave him a version of events. Maxwell said that the victim was an Italian police agent who had been sent to London to infiltrate a gang of revolutionaries. He succeeded, posing as one of them and lived at Cranbourne Street in Soho. Unfortunately for him, he kept his written instructions in his pockets. His fellows waited until he was asleep and searched his clothes and found these notes. They then lay in wait for him and stunned the man. He was taken to the cellar where he regained consciousness. He was then stabbed to death and then they tried to dispose of the body by fire. This took too long, so they chopped up the body and then took it to the Thames. This meets the facts, such as they are, but cannot be verified and it also smacks of being too good a story told by a not necessarily reliable source before being recounted by the retired policeman in his memoirs.

The answer to this brutal murder will probably be never known. It leaves behind it a number of questions which can never be satis-factorily answered. On the part of the killer(s), though, it was a great success.

CHAPTER 8

The Murder of Emma Jackson 1863

I think the girl with the round hat who walks Oxford Street told him that I have been with other men and he is so jealous that he swears he will take my life. If ever I am murdered, that is the man who would do it.

St Giles was 'one of the worst neighbourhoods in the metropolis' stated *The Times* in 1863. In the previous year, a cab driver accosted his fare there, a young woman, and not content with robbing and stripping her, he then tried to force her into a brothel. However, in April 1863, there was to be an even more heinous crime.

Emma Jackson, aged twenty-eight, was no stranger to vice. She lived with her father, an out of work clerk, above a butcher's shop in Berwick Street, Soho, and her mother, a shirt maker. Like her mother, she made shirts, but she also made money as a prostitute. Then she would be absent from home for some days.

On Tuesday 7 April, she left home, returning there on the following day for what was to be the last time. On the morning of Thursday 9 April, she was seen with a man on the corner of Dean Street and Old Compton Street. Daniel Murphy, a young boot black, polished their shoes. He recalled that the man 'spoke good English' and was:

> ... *about twenty-five years old, five feet six high, fair hair and complexion, a little whiskers round all over his face but not much, no moustache, dress: wide awake, black overcoat with bob tail coat underneath, black trousers, kid leather boots, side springs, new, and no shirt collar, dark tie.*

The two then went to a lodging house cum brothel on George Street a little later in the morning. They knocked on the door and it was opened by Margaret Curley, a servant employed at the place. Emma said they wanted a room for two hours. This was not an

Berwick Street, Soho, 2006. Emma Jackson's home was on this street. Author's collection

unusual request there, as people appeared at all hours of the day or night, wanting accommodation. She let them in and took them to a room on the first floor. They entered, shook up the bed and said it would do. The man gave her a shilling. Margaret could not remember much about the man because she was still rather sleepy.

> *The man who came in with the deceased I did not see go away. I have no idea when he went. I cannot describe him beyond that he is of the middle height and dressed in dark clothes.*

This sounds like the same man who was seen by the lad only a little earlier.

At 11.30 am, Margaret rose from her renewed slumbers and told the manager of the place, Mr George, about the transaction and gave him the shilling. After that, no one paid any heed to the occupants of the room until about 5.00pm in the evening. Margaret asked Clara Mullinde, a twenty-year-old prostitute who stayed at the house, to see what was going on. She did so and Margaret later stated, 'She came down the stairs screaming "There's a woman dead in the room"'.

Dr John Weekes arrived with the police and saw the frightful scene – Emma's corpse lay on the bed, its throat cut and the walls and bed were spattered with blood. According to *The Times*:

He found that, in addition to the windpipe having been severed enough of itself to cause death, there was another wound severing the carotid artery, and on the back of the neck two large stab wounds running obliquely towards each other. All the wounds had been inflicted with great force.

No one at the house knew much about the murder. Thomas Connor, an elderly hawker, who lodged there, had been awake from about 7.00 to 9.00 that morning and had not heard or seen anything suspicious. The other occupants of the place, from the owner (who slept immediately beneath the room where the murder was committed) to the servants and lodgers, also said that they had seen nothing out of the ordinary. The street in which the house was located was a quiet one and there was little in the way of traffic which traversed it.

The inquest took place on the day following the murder. The corpse had not been moved and so all the jury were obliged to visit the den of ill repute and to witness the corpse in situ. John Jackson, Emma's brother, identified the body and said he had not seen her since Sunday. He had no idea where she was in those days nor who she was with. It was thought that very little struggle could have taken place because two girls slept in the adjacent room and heard nothing – the plaster wall was so thin that even voices in low tones could be heard from one room to another.

Weekes explained a little more of what he had seen when he arrived at the scene on the previous day. The corpse was lying on its back on the bed, almost naked. He thought that the throat had been cut first, as some of the other wounds might not have killed her, or at least would have allowed her to cry out, which it seemed she did not do. Suicide was ruled out due to the lack of a weapon being found and to the nature of the wounds. She had been dead since 11.00 am in the morning, possibly earlier.

The inquest was then adjourned until 17 April. By this time, Weekes had had more time in which to carry out a post-mortem. He recounted how he had found blood on the limbs and the buttocks, but the cause of death was due to suffocation and loss of blood. He thought that Emma had been asleep when she was killed. Once the first blow had been struck to the neck, no noise would be made. A common pocket knife had been used to kill and the killer must have been spattered with blood.

There were a number of possibilities as to who the murderer was. One of Emma's friends thought the man was a foreigner, perhaps a German baker or a sugar baker, judging by his appearance. Charlotte Bradshaw claimed to have been one of Emma's friends and told the police that, at Easter, Emma had been with one Leon Prusien, a German baker from Peckham, and this man told Emma, 'Now you know me, if ever I see you with anyone I will have your life' and then sprang at her with a knife, wounding Charlotte, who intervened. Yet the police were doubtful. They went with Charlotte to Peckham and saw a number of German bakers, none of whom could be identified, and they wondered if Charlotte had known Emma at all.

Sarah Jackson, Emma's sister-in-law, had seen Emma six weeks before. Emma had been to a house in Right Street, saying, 'I only want to see my man who lives there.' The door had been locked, so she said, 'I can't get in. I suspect his damned woman is there.' She then explained, 'I think the girl with the round hat who walks Oxford Street told him that I have been with other men and he is so jealous that he swears he will take my life. If ever I am murdered, that is the man who would do it.' Apparently this unnamed man had been violent towards her already. He had good reason to be jealous as Emma had been with a man on Monday, according to one of the others at the house in George Street.

Another suspect was a man who entered a shop in Stratford on the day of the murder and who purchased a new shirt – the one he was wearing being stained with blood. When being asked by the shop-

Peckham, c.1905. Police questioned a number of Germans here over Sarah's murder. Author's collection

keeper, the man said that he had had a quarrel with his wife, which had turned violent. He then left in the direction of Epping Forest and was thought to be in hiding there. He was described as being 'About forty years of age, five foot six inches in height, fresh complexion, rather weather beaten, dark sandy whiskers, clean shaved under the chin. Wore a pilot coat buttoned close up to the chin.' This sounds like a different man to that identified by the boot black.

Or was the killer the man who drowned himself in the Thames in the following month? An unknown man, respectably dressed, aged about thirty, was found floating off the St Katharine Docks by Richard Reilly, a customs man. The corpse seemed to be of an Englishman, not a foreigner, who had tied his hands together by twine. He wore brown and grey crossed tweed clothes, with a red shirt, white collar and black tie. He had few possessions and no money. Nor was a knife was found on his person. The key witnesses were shown the corpse, but none made any positive identification. They said that the features were too distorted by the water to be certain. Inspector Williamson commented, 'There was nothing to lead to the belief that this was the man but the supposed resemblance'. This recalls Montague John Druitt, who committed suicide by drowning himself in the Thames in December 1888 and who was subsequently accused of being Jack the Ripper. Dead men are easy to blame as they cannot give an account of themselves.

In the following weeks, months and years, a number of men were suspected, mostly on account of the police having circulated descriptions of the wanted man all around the country. Anyone who resembled him was brought in for questioning by the local police and detectives from London were travelling all around the British Isles to question these men.

One such was Thomas Riley, who was arrested at Cardiff on 23 April. He had seemed confused and uneasy when Emma Jackson's name had been mentioned. Yet he was found to have been in Limerick Prison from 2 to 17 April, so could not have been guilty. One Louis Smith, arrested in Glasgow, was another suspect. He was a German by birth and tried to commit suicide.

There were also confessions and letters sent to the police. Edward Connell confessed to the murder in 1864. He was given to drink, was insane and violent, but was not identified by the principal witness, Murphy, so was discharged. Seven years later, William Squires, a shoemaker in his thirties, confessed. He was a habitual criminal and another drunk. But with no evidence against him, he too was discharged. A letter from America claimed that one Whitton, who had killed himself there in 1866, was the killer. Again, there was no proof. A sailor at the Chatham dockyards was accused. Finally, a soldier serving in India in 1873 was said to know a lot about the murder, especially when he was in his cups.

The murder was never solved. In all probability, Emma was killed by her violent lover, to whom she had referred when talking to her sister-in-law, but never named. This may well have been due to his jealousy and controlling nature. The crime was easy as she trusted him and when she was asleep he slit her throat before inflicting other wounds on her. He then escaped, probably by merely walking out of the house when the coast was clear. Perhaps he had a little luck. Emma certainly had none.

CHAPTER 9

The Deadly Caller
1866

That is a very serious charge indeed:
I am as innocent as a baby.

Mrs Sarah Millson, aged fifty-one, had worked for Messrs Bevington, wholesale leather merchants, of Cannon Street, for a decade. She was the housekeeper. Her fellow servant, Elizabeth Lowes, the cook, had also worked for the firm for that length of time. Sarah's husband, Edwin, had been employed as a warehouseman and had died six years previously. The two women slept in separate rooms and Elizabeth thought that Sarah was cheerful. Miss Cox, a young friend of Sarah's, often visited, as did her sister, but she had few male callers, save a short, dark man about two or three years before, and no admirers ever visited, as far as was known.

On the evening of Wednesday 11 April 1866, their lives were to change forever. Sarah let Edward Kipps, an employee of the firm, out of the premises at 7.50 pm. He was always the last man to leave of the evening and did all the locking up. Sarah told Elizabeth that the building was now empty, apart from themselves. At 8.50 pm, the door bell rang. Sarah came into the dining room, which was on the second floor, and announced, 'That's for me', and went downstairs to answer it. This was at the front door, which was fastened from within. Elizabeth remained in the dining room. Because the front door was separated from the dining room by a lobby and a pair of glass swing doors, before a passageway leading to the stairs was reached, Elizabeth could hear nothing more of what occurred downstairs near the entrance.

Elizabeth stayed where she was for over an hour, before going downstairs at about 10.15 pm. It was not uncommon for Sarah to stay downstairs after having answered the door. But before she reached the foot of the steps, she saw a grim sight. Sarah was lying on her back with her feet towards the stairs and her head towards the glass doors. Her face was covered with blood. Elizabeth took her hand and called her name, but there was no response. She dashed from the building to find a constable.

When she had opened the door, she saw a young woman standing by the building, sheltering from the rain. Elizabeth asked the woman to come inside and that someone had suffered a fit. The woman said, 'Oh dear me, I can't come in', and then ran down the street. Finally a policeman came into sight and, after seeing the body, went to the nearest police station to fetch further help.

Mr May, a surgeon, examined the body. There were twelve wounds on the face and head. These included four stabs to the face, one on the forehead and one on the left side of the head. The eyes were swollen and the nose was blackened. A heavy piece of iron, possibly a crow bar, may have been used. Although there were some tools nearby, including a crowbar, chisel and a hammer, these were clean. Yet there was a missing crowbar; possibly the murder weapon. There was no sign of a struggle and her clothes had not been disarranged.

What the motive could have been was unclear. It was almost certainly not attempted robbery, either from the premises or from Sarah personally. Mr Bevington said that nothing in the counting house or the warehouse had been disturbed. Elizabeth did not think Sarah had much in the way of savings.

It was then discovered that Sarah was in debt to George Terry, an associate of a moneylender, through whom one Mrs Webber had lent her £30. Falling into financial troubles himself, Terry was living in Southwark. There he met one William Smith, and told him of the unpaid debt. Smith resolved to obtain the money for him. The two went to the street where she lived and Terry told Smith exactly where Sarah was to be found.

A letter from Terry had been found among Sarah's possessions after her death. It read:

> *Mrs Millson, – the bearer of this I have sent to you as my adviser. I have taken this course as I have received so much annoyance from Mrs Webber that I can put up with it no longer. He will propose terms to you which you may accept or not, at your pleasure. Failing your agreeing to this proposal he is instructed by me to see Mr Bevington or Mr Harris and explain to them how the matter stands. You know yourself what reasons you put forward for borrowing the money (doctors' bills and physicians for your husband) which you know was not so. I shall also have him bring your sister before Mr Bevington, if necessary, or your obstinacy compels my adviser to go to the extreme. I am yours obediently, GEORGE TERRY*

Smith had been to see Sarah early in 1866 and had received £1 from her but had made subsequent visits, which had distressed her (despite Elizabeth's earlier declaration about Sarah's cheerfulness), leading

Cannon Street. Sarah Millson was murdered here. John Coulter's collection

her to borrow money from Elizabeth. It was this letter which led to Smith's arrest.

So, a week after the murder, the police took in Smith, who lived in Eton, on suspicion of being the killer. Smith was described as 'a tall, athletic young man of about twenty-five and was dressed in a black frock coat and drab trousers'. When he was arrested, he was asked when he was last in London and he claimed it was on 10 January, with his mother. When his mother was asked his whereabouts for the night of the murder, she said she did not know the answer, but that he returned very late. The house was searched and clothing spotted with blood was found.

Smith protested his innocence when charged with murder. He said:

> *That is a very serious charge indeed: I am as innocent as a baby. I have not been in London since the 1st of February, when I called upon a Mr Fuggle at 10. Aldermanbury, about some money that is due to me. My brother lent him £10. I first went with that letter (the letter signed George Terry) the latter part of last year. I called about 3 o'clock in the afternoon. She was washing up the things. I believe it was either Thursday or Friday the first time that I went. She told me to come on Saturday, and I called on the Saturday.*

He agreed that he had collected money from her; 2 sovereigns on a total of three occasions, for which he had signed receipts; one of these having been found amongst Sarah's possessions. Smith's movements were unclear on the fatal night. He claimed to be with Mr Harris, a hatter of Eton, until 7.30 pm, but local police could only say that they had seen him in Eton between midnight and 1.00 am.

The inquest concluded on 25 April. Mrs Arabella Robbins, a young widow, living in Cannon Street, gave fresh evidence. She thought she saw Smith leaving the premises at 9.50 pm, after violently slamming the door behind him, though she admitted she did not have a complete glimpse of his face from the front. Yet she did pick him out of an identity parade of fourteen men. Catherine Collins, Mrs Robbins's servant, recalled seeing Smith a few months previously as well as on the night of the murder. Another witness said he had seen Smith at Bevington's warehouse on an earlier occasion. He recalled Smith asking for either Sarah or Elizabeth; he could not recall which.

George Terry was then summoned. He and Smith had been in the same lodgings the previous year. Smith talked of the money he was due and Terry mentioned that he needed money from Sarah to repay Mrs Webber. Smith said, 'I'll get it for you; I'll manage that.' After Smith had been shown where Sarah lived, Smith visited her and then gave some money (14 shillings) to Terry, who gave him 5 shillings for his trouble.

May, the surgeon, then told the court the cause of death. This was not the fracture of the skull, but extensive effusion of blood. The blows were of great violence.

The coroner then summed up. There was no doubt that Smith was in the habit of visiting Sarah in order to extract money from her, nor that she had been killed on the same night that Mrs Robbins claimed

Eton, c.1904. William Smith, who was tried for Susan's murder, lived here. Author's collection

she saw him leave the premises. The circumstantial evidence against Smith was very strong indeed. He was committed for trial on the evidence which had been collected.

Montague Williams, Smith's counsel, said that Smith had been seen at 7.45 on the Slough Road, so could not possibly have reached Cannon Street in time to have committed the crime. That was assuming the train to Paddington had arrived on time.

One Frank Russell told the police that he was willing to disclose 'a very curious circumstance relating to the murder in Cannon Street'. He said he knew that one Miss Ann Newman, who worked in Oppenheim's factory in Blackfriars, had valuable evidence. Russell claimed that she had said she 'was not surprised that the woman was murdered in Cannon Street as she once gave evidence against a man who was transported and he had returned to London four days prior to the murder'. Ann denied she ever made this statement and related how a girl she knew had surmised that a male friend of the deceased was responsible for the murder.

There was also a letter of confession, brought by one John Tutill of Bermondsey, who had found it in Westmorland Road in Walworth, which read as follows:

I alone and unaided did murder Mrs Millson at Cannon Street West and that I did it half past nine o'clock at night and that the cook must have heard it if you want to find the right one you must go to the house and call for Taylor.

The police treated it thus, 'It appears to be the act of an insane person, or one who writes with the view of misleading the police'.

Smith was put on trial at the Old Bailey on 13 June. All the witnesses who had previously given evidence appeared, as well as additional ones, such as Miss Cox and Amelia Long, who said that they had seen Smith visit Sarah on previous occasions. Elizabeth said that Sarah did a great deal of writing and received numerous letters. Various men said that they had seen him in the early evening of 11 April, going towards the railway station. The 7.43 pm train from Slough would take an hour to arrive at Paddington, explained a railway official. Smith could then have caught a train from there to the City – they ran every five or ten minutes. Yet, if Smith was trying to catch the train from Slough, and he was not running, it would have meant that he would have had to cover over a mile in thirteen minutes; the Windsor station would have been more convenient as it was far closer.

The case for the defence was that Sarah saw other people when she went downstairs to the door on other occasions; she did not only see Smith there, who had, after all, only called three times. It was suggested that she had a skeleton in her cupboard, but as to who and what, there was now no clue. It was said that the letters written to and from her were from a potentially dangerous acquaintance. Finally, it was asked why should Smith kill her? He was receiving the money from her as desired.

There were a number of witnesses who said that they saw Smith on the evening of the murder in Eton. Harris said he met Smith in Eton Square at 8.20 pm. They then went for a walk and visited a beer house until after 10.00. A policeman later told Harris's father that he had seen Smith on Windsor Bridge at 11.10 pm. A number of other men recalled seeing Smith in Eton between 7.00 and 9.00 pm. Thus the defence summed up that numerous witnesses could provide Smith with an alibi.

The question was whether it was certain that the man seen leaving the house was Smith. If so, he was the killer. But witnesses had erred in identifying suspects in the past. Mrs Robbins had only seen the man for a brief time. If there was reasonable doubt, argued the judge, the jury must give the accused the benefit of it. They did so, and Smith left the courtroom a free man.

Eight years later, one Eliza Croft, the wife of a labourer in Erith, who was suffering from depression, thought that her uncle, Edward

Pope, was the killer. Apparently he had spoken in his sleep of the murder in 1872 and he and Eliza's mother had begged her not to mention this to the police. Despite an investigation into his previous employment and whereabouts in 1866, it was felt that too many years had passed. Finding evidence and reliable witnesses would be impossible, and so, after questioning, nothing else happened.

One question which was never answered, or enquired about, was the woman whom Elizabeth saw just outside the door. Had she seen anything and then been too frightened to speak to anyone about it? It seems Smith was probably innocent, because he had no motive to kill and was receiving a form of commission on the money he was taking from her. The question to ask is whether Sarah's financial worries had anything to do with her murder, or whether they were completely separate from them. Who was she in correspondence with? If we knew that, then we might be nearer her killer, for it was almost certainly someone she knew and probably arranged to meet.

Chapter 10

The Mystery of Edmund Pook 1871

Let me die.

The seventeen-year-old Jane Maria Clousen, whose father was a night watchman in Deptford, had been employed by Mr Pook, a stationer of London Street, Greenwich, as a servant for two years. Her employment there had come to an end on 13 April 1871, for reasons which are obscure, and she had subsequently lived with the family of Fanny Hamilton, a friend, at Ashburnham Road, Greenwich. Fanny later said that her friend was in low spirits, but not why.

On the evening of Tuesday 25 April 1871, she had left the house with Fanny at 6.00 pm and they had walked to Deptford. The two parted at the junction of Douglas Street and Deptford High Street. Fanny went back home. She never saw Jane alive again. The time was 6.37 pm. Was it significant that Jane had earlier asked Fanny the time? One account states that Jane told her friend, 'I am going to see Ned, he has sent for me.'

PC Donald Gunn was on duty on the lonely Kidbrooke Lane that night. He passed along the lane at about 1.45 am on the morning of 26 April, but neither saw nor heard anything untoward. However, when he returned about an hour and a half later, he found a dying woman on the side of the lane, whom he later discovered to be Jane. She was moaning piteously and had been badly injured to the head. There were fourteen wounds on her, including the fatal blow to the forehead which had shattered part of the skull. Gunn approached her and she fell flat on her face, saying, 'Let me die'.

The ground nearby was soft and footprints and blood were clearly visible, as were her hat and gloves. A locket was found on her person. A metal whistle was also found on the scene. The footprints were partly effaced by the dew and seemed to point in all directions. In any case, no steps were taken to preserve these. When Gunn's colleague, Sergeant Haynes arrived, he noticed bloodstains 300 yards away, on both sides of the Lower Kidbrooke stream which crossed the lane, possibly made by whoever made the footprints away from the body in that direction.

Kidbrooke Lane, c.1890. The scene of Jane Clousen's murder. Author's collection

Jane's body was taken to Dr Michael Harris of Guy's Hospital. She was unconscious and very cold. He found fourteen wounds to the face and head and others to the arms and hands, probably caused when she had tried to defend herself from her assailant. Part of the skull had been smashed, as had the jaw bone, and the brain was lacerated. She died on 30 April. It was probable that the sharp edges of a hammer had caused these wounds. Harris also discovered that she was two months pregnant.

On 27 April, Thomas Brown, a gardener at Morden College, found a plasterer's hammer in the college grounds, not far from the foot-path. It was rusty, but bloodstains were also found upon it. This was probably the murder weapon. Yet the motive for the murder was unclear. Jane had not been robbed (her purse contained 11s 4d), nor had she been ravished.

William Trott, Jane's uncle, identified the body and presumably told the police a little about her recent employment history. Super-intendent Griffin and Inspector Mulvany paid a visit to the house of Jane's late employer. Mr Pook's son, the twenty-year-old Edmund Pook, a printer, was also present. He had a local reputation as a flirt and a would-be ladies' man. Mulvany told the young man they wanted to ask him a few questions about Jane. He agreed, but claimed he had not seen her since she left his father's employment and that she was 'a very dirty young woman', whereas her friends spoke of Jane as

Morden College, Blackheath, c.1905. The alleged murder weapon was found in the college grounds. Author's collection

being 'clean, respectable ... hardworking'. A former employer, Mr Taylor of Ashburnham Grove, Greenwich, spoke glowingly of Jane, 'a clever, more civil or quieter girl never could be inside a house', and thought she had been 'clean and respectable' since. The police told Pook that Jane's friends claimed he had written to her, but he did not recall that he had. His father said this was nonsense, implying as it did that his son had formed an attachment with Jane.

Edmund was then asked to account for his movements on the night of the murder. He said that he went to see a young lady in Lewisham that evening, but had not been able to see her, and was home for 8.45 pm. The shirt he had worn on that night was shown to have a bloodstain on the right wristband. This may have been caused by a cut on his left arm by a machine at the printworks, but the police thought otherwise and saw this as conclusive proof against the young man. He was arrested but went willingly, remarking, 'Very well; I'll go with you anywhere'. He took a copy of *The Pickwick Papers* with him to read whilst awaiting trial – he had to spend four weeks in Maidstone Gaol.

He latter contradicted his earlier statement that he had not seen Jane since her dismissal and told the police that he had seen Jane with a well-dressed man on the Saturday evening before her death. If this was true, then it was a piece of crucial news, but was not apparently followed up.

The trial of Edmund Pook took place at the Old Bailey over four days, 12–15 July. Unusually the jury was not made up of anyone from Kent, such was the prejudice there against him. The case for the prosecution was as follows. Jane left Fanny Hamilton with the intention of meeting Pook. Second, Pook was later seen in Greenwich, hot and bothered, having had enough time to have met Jane and then returned. Third, a man similar to Pook had been seen hurrying along Kidbrooke Lane on the evening of 25 April. Fourth, blood had been found on Pook's shirt. Fifth, he had been trying to buy a hammer on the day before the murder. Sixth, he had lied about his whereabouts on the night of the murder and on the previous night, claiming he was in London, whereas he was not. Finally he had made an appointment to see Miss Durnford in Lewisham on 27 April, though without saying he had tried to see her two days previously.

To elaborate: William Sparshott, an ironmonger on Deptford High Street, said Pook asked him for an axe on the evening of 24 April, as he said he needed one for a play. Pook often took part in amateur dramatics. Sparshott offered him a cook's chopper for 2s 2d, but Pook said it was too dear and he left without buying it. Sparshott picked out Pook from a police identity parade. Mrs Thomas, who kept an ironmonger's shop across the road, did sell a cheaper hammer on that night, but did not recollect to whom.

William Norton, a coachman, said that he had been walking along Kidbrooke Lane on the evening of 25 April, with Louisa Putnam. He saw a young couple there at about 8.30 pm. He later heard a scream and saw the man running along the lane towards Kidbrooke. How-

Deptford High Street. It was alleged that Pook bought the murder weapon here. John Coulter's collection

High Street, Deptford

ever, he thought that the scream was merely a playful scream, rather than one of pain or anguish. When he and his companion walked towards the source of the noise, they saw no one there. He could not identify Pook as the man. William Cronk also saw a couple on the pathway, but thought he heard the woman refer to her companion as 'Charlie' and said either 'let us go' or 'let me go'. Although he picked out Pook, this was on the basis of his clothes, as he did not see the man's face.

Alice Durnford of Bridge Place, Lewisham, told the court that she had known Pook for eighteen months and they did meet occasionally. She knew that Pook did have a whistle similar to the one found at the scene of the crime. However, these were very common and Pook could account for both his whistles. Furthermore, although the locket found there was thought to have been given to Jane by Pook, it turned out to have been given to her by one Humphries, a man who worked for Pook's father.

John Barr, a Greenwich pawnbroker, said he was walking with Miss Priscilla Billington on the evening of 25 April. They had been walking up Royal Hill and saw Pook near Circus Street in Greenwich. He was walking quickly. The time was just before 9.00 pm. Mrs Ellen Plane, who kept a confectioners on Royal Hill recalled that Pook came into the shop shortly afterwards. He was hot and excited and claimed to have run from Lewisham. He asked her for a brush so he could clean his clothes. He then left and walked the short distance to his father's house.

Further witnesses made the case against Pook seem worse. Thomas Lazell, a gardener and florist of Kidbrooke Lane, said that he saw Pook on the 25 April, at about 6.50 pm. They were about 300 yards from the lane. Pook was with a woman and his arm around her waist. Yet this woman could not have been Jane as she was at Deptford at 6.37 pm.

Dr Henry Lethby had found bloodstains on Pook's trousers and a hair which was similar to Jane's. Yet, such was the primitive state of science that it was impossible to tell whether the hairs were from the same person, nor when the stains were made, or whether they were human or animal blood, let alone whose.

It was now the turn of the defence. Mr Huddleston, QC, addressed the jury on Pook's behalf. He said there was absolutely no reason why Pook should kill Jane. There was only the suggestion that Pook had seduced Jane whilst she was in his father's employ, but there was no proof of this. Huddleston said the two had never been seen together and claimed that the police had been assuming too much on too little evidence, which had often occurred in the past. However, Emily

Wolledge, who also lived with Fanny Hamilton and Jane, said that there was known familiarity between Pook and Jane.

He also questioned the assumption that the murder occurred at about 8.30 pm, when Norton heard the scream and saw the man running. It was more likely that the murder was committed in the early hours of the following day, probably shortly before the policeman found the body. He also argued that the bloodspots on Pook's clothing were relatively trivial and that whoever killed Jane must have been covered with blood, so horrific were her injuries, and none who saw him later that day remarked on them. Huddleston thought that it had not been proved that Pook had been in the vicinity of Kidbrooke Lane and that Lazell, who did not know Pook very well, was mistaken. In any case, it was two and a half miles from there to the shop in which Pook was later seen. He could not have been the man seen there.

After having demolished, as he thought, the case for the prosecution, he then moved onto the defence proper. Huddleston said that the blood spots might have been the result of epileptic fits which Pook suffered from. Thomas Pook, Pook's brother, said that his brother had gone to Lewisham to try and see Miss Durnford, after finishing work (at Douglas Street, Deptford) at 7.00 pm and leaving home about twenty-five minutes later. Pook had waited by the railway station for forty minutes, returning home just after 9.00 pm. Witnesses had seen him in Lewisham Road between 8.00 and 9.00 pm. They included one Miss Eliza Merritt, who thought he was waiting for someone. Edward McKenzie, a fireman, recalled seeing Pook on the morning of the murder and noticed that Pook already had some blood spots on his clothes. Lazell's story about seeing Pook was also questioned, as he had apparently told someone that he had not seen anyone on the lane on the night of the murder. In any case, Pook was still at work at 6.50 pm. Lazell could not have seen him at that time. Therefore, Pook had not been in the vicinity of Kidbrooke Lane that evening. He could not have committed the murder. Nor could it be proved he purchased a deadly weapon on the evening before the murder.

The murder was, as the prosecution stated, 'a planned, cold-blooded, deliberate murder'. The judge summed up this complex case in Pook's favour, pointing out the inconsistencies in the prosecution's case. After retiring for twenty minutes, the jury found him to be not guilty. Pook walked away, a free man. Not all thought he was innocent – a crowd demonstrated outside the family home, enraged at the acquittal. He was even burnt in effigy by the crowd in Deptford. Pook and his family tried to clear his name from any imputation of the crime, but this was inconclusive and raised further popular animus against him. Generally speaking, the poorer people thought him

'Tourists' flock to the scene of the murder at Eltham, 1871. Copy supplied by Mike Egan

guilty and the middle classes thought him innocent. As for Pook, he remained in Greenwich, working in the family business, which he took over after his father's death. He himself died in Croydon in 1920.

The case against Pook had been largely circumstantial and based on suggestions about what might have happened, without much proof. He was the police's only suspect and they had convinced themselves he was guilty and had not looked for anyone else (not an uncommon line of official reasoning). The questions to be asked are: who seduced Jane and was that man her murderer? The answer is probably yes, unless she was killed by a random murderer. Could Mr Humphries, a shadowy figure, who does not seem to have been investigated, but who was clearly attracted to Jane – hence the gift of the locket – have had a larger role in the case? Possibly not, because there was the man who Pook saw Jane with on the Saturday before the murder, and whom he did not identify – and he would have known Humphries as he worked for his father. Clearly Jane went to Kidbrooke Lane to meet a man; someone who may have written to her to arrange a rendezvous. Yet the meeting was in the evening and she was not found until early next morning. Presumably she had stayed out all night with the man she met, whom she clearly trusted and thought meant her well. This sounds like her seducer who promised to help her out of her dilemma, either by marriage or with a substantial financial gift, perhaps. Or perhaps Jane's intention was blackmail. The truth will never be known. Unfortunately his intention in meeting her was completely different to that which she envisaged. The scandal that might have enveloped him out of their association was one that he thought he could only deal with by murder.

CHAPTER 11

Murder for Christmas 1872

... it had been conclusively shown that Dr Hessel was not the companion of Harriet Burswell on the night of the murder.

Christmas is usually hailed as the season of peace on Earth and goodwill towards all men. The reality is often very different from these hopes and this story illustrates it only too well.

Harriet Buswell, also known as Clara Burton, was twenty-seven years old in 1872 and was a ballet dancer. Given the low wages she was paid, she supplemented her income as many dancers did, by prostitution. At the time of her death she had clothing pawned and some of her jewellery was borrowed. She had spent the evening of 24 December 1872 with a man. They had been to the Hotel Cavour for dinner and to the Alhambra. At about 12.30 am on the following day, they went back to her room, which was on the second floor of a house in Great Coram Street in Bloomsbury (now Coram Street). She paid Harriet Wright, her landlady, half a sovereign as the rent was owing, and received a shilling change. She then went to her room where her companion was waiting for her and was never seen alive again by anyone else.

Her companion was heard leaving the house a few hours later. Because nothing was heard of Harriet by the late morning, the locked door of her room was burst open. A shocking sight lay before them. Harriet was lying on the bed. Her throat had been cut, either by herself or another. The police were called just after 1.00 pm that Christmas afternoon. Superintendent Thomson, an experienced officer, accompanied by a detective sergeant, set about the inquiry to find her killer, and did not summon the detective force, deciding that his men would be able to succeed without calling in the 'experts'.

The body was examined. There were two stab wounds on the corpse, one under the left ear and the other on the left of the windpipe

Alhambra Theatre. Harriet Buswell dined here with her final client. John Coulter's collection

'large enough to put a man's fist in'. The knife used to inflict these wounds was probably a clasp knife. There was the mark of a bloody thumb on the forehead, indicating that the killer had held the head down whilst the second blow was inflicted. The right hand of the victim was raised, as if in a feeble effort to ward off the blow. The body was removed to St Giles workhouse where it was identified by her brother on the following day.

Then there were a few clues in the room itself. Harriet's earrings and purse were missing. Yet these were of little value – the earrings being only worth 5 shillings. Perhaps the killer thought that his victim, living in a fairly well-to-do district, would have possessions worth taking. The door key was also missing – the door having been locked from the outside. Thomson also noticed that the window had not been opened.

On the table near to the window, there was an oil lamp, half full. There was a perfectly clean washstand in the room. Under it was a small jug of water, which had the appearance of someone's hands having been washed in it. Added to this there was a towel, damp and stained with blood. There were also bloodstains on the towel, indicative of a knife being wiped there. Bags of fruit were found, as were some of the deceased's papers. These letters did not provide much information; they were from a number of correspondents –

Harriet's sister, one Charles who had met her several times and William Kirby of Hong Kong, who had been in love with her,

A little of Harriet's life story was revealed. She had been born in Wisbech and her father had been a tailor. Both parents died about ten years before. Harriet had five siblings. One brother lived in Norwich, another in London and others in Sussex. Harriet had come down to London and originally worked as a servant in Finchley in 1863. A coachman of the name of Burton seduced her, dying shortly afterwards, but leaving Harriet with a child (Kate, born in 1864 and at a 'nice school' in 1872). She later lived with a Major Brown at Nelson Square, then Stamford Street, giving birth to two stillborn children. She lived in a number of addresses in London over the next few years. It was in 1870 that she had met Kirby, now in Hong Kong, who sent her money (£60 in total) and advice from there, asking her to desist from prostitution. In the following year, Harriet lived with Kate and one of her sisters in Sussex, but returned to London later that year.

It was soon clear that the inmates of the house were all innocent. However, there were witnesses to hand. Mary Neston, a servant, had been on her way to work that morning and had seen the man leaving the house at about 7.15 am. She gave a description:

He is about twenty-five years of age, five feet nine inches high, with neither beard, whiskers, nor moustache but not having shaved for two or three days, his beard when grown would be rather dark. He has a swarthy complexion, and blotches or pimples on his face. He was dressed in dark clothes, and wore a dark brown overcoat down to his knees, billycock hat, and rather heavy boots.

It was also thought that he would have blood on his clothes after such a bloody murder, though as noted, he probably washed this off his hands whilst in Harriet's room.

The Home Secretary decreed that a reward of £100 would be given to anyone who could identify the killer. This was doubled in January.

Another witness, a grocer called George Flack, recalled seeing Harriet and her companion just after midnight when they purchased some fruit from his shop. The man paid for 9 pence worth, but refused Harriet's request that he buy her some grapes. Flack thought that the way the man said 'No' showed him to be a German.

The inquest took place in three sittings over January 1873. In this period a man was arrested at Bushey in Hertfordshire on 14 January. He was drunk and told the police that he was of German and French stock. He confessed to the murder. However on the following day, he denied everything he had said. Following the failure of a witness to

Piccadilly, London.

Piccadilly, c.1900. Harriet and her client travelled along Piccadilly. Author's collection

identify him, he was released. Another suspect was a young Frenchman, Georges Maudeuit, who was found dead by natural causes in his lodgings in Church Street, Soho. Some of the witnesses recognized him as the man they had seen with Harriet, but others did not.

The public certainly seemed well disposed to help the police. Thomson had received almost 300 letters about the case. Some were from people who thought they had seen the criminal. There was a sighting on 31 January of a man at Epping Station and a tramp seen at Micheldever resembled the description of the killer in some respects. A landlady near Birmingham saw a German customer in her pub, and later read about the murder in the *Birmingham Post*. Others gave what they deemed to be helpful hints. One Allen Franklin thought the killer had 'a lonely occupation and skilled, leaving the man entirely to his own thoughts and reserve, and thereby throwing off all suspicion'. 'Justice', writing from Oxford said that the killer's nationality was more likely to be Italian or French, given his swarthy complexion, must be reasonably well off to treat Harriet and so probably lived in private lodgings. None of these letters, doubtless all well meant, seemed to have helped, though.

There were a number of witnesses who had information to give before the coroner, and these were accorded far more weight. Walter Darling, an omnibus conductor, remembered taking the fares of a couple just after midnight on 25 December. They got on at Piccadilly Circus and alighted at Judd Street, or so he believed. He thought that the man was wearing an Alpine hat – a felt one turned up at the sides and the top knocked down. He could not be certain if the man was a foreigner or not.

Mary Neston was the next to speak, and much of her evidence has already been stated. But she added, with all the wisdom born from hindsight, 'I thought there was something wrong'. Asked why this was the case, she replied, 'Because, when he found himself opposite me, he turned his face round as if he did not want to be seen and he turned his shoulders round too.' The man then walked towards Brunswick Square. Mary had never seen him before.

One man who knew Harriet well was George Studdart, residing at the Drummond Hotel and a student at the Royal Veterinary College. He had known her by the name of Clara Burton and had first met her at the Alhambra and had been with her to her room in Great Coram Street. He had not seen her since 8 December and claimed to know nothing about the murder. He did not believe she was threatened by anyone. Although he paid her for services rendered, he did know that a man in Hong Kong sent her large sums of money at intervals. Studdart had known Harriet since October, but must have felt close to her, because he said that, if he was ill, she was to be called for.

He did recall an argument taking place at the Alhambra. A large man had pushed against Studdart and had then wanted to fight him. Studdart must have been drunk at the time as his only knowledge of the incident was what Harriet had told him on the following day. The argument was over Harriet. It was claimed that he had once returned home with blood on his clothes and had remarked that some day Harriet would be killed by ill-disposed persons. Studdart denied he had ever spoken such words.

Studdart had an alibi for the time of the murder. He had left London for Ireland on the Friday before Christmas and had not returned until January. Thomson had clearly investigated this as he added that the student had been seen in Ireland on 24–26 December.

Charles Boardman, who supplied goods on credit, had done business with Harriet. He visited her once a week to collect the money she owed him. On death her debt was £5 10s to him and he had last seen her on 16 December. He thought that she was leading a 'gay' life; in other words, one which needed constant funds. But she was usually able to make payments to him, often £1 a week, or at least 5s. Harriet had told him that she was on the brink of a better standard of living when they last met.

More was learnt of Harriet's life. In 1871–2, she had lodged with Emma Wilson of Argyle Street, at the rate of 30s a week for board and

Coram Street, 2006. Harriet Buswell was killed in her room in this street. Author's collection

lodging. Emma and Harriet were on good terms. There was never any problem about the rent being paid. Yet she was £9 in debt to Emma when she left her, owing to a falling out over Emma's telling her she did not look after Kate properly. Harriet had had clients visit her, but they never caused any trouble and Harriet was rarely drunk. Harriet's relatives sometimes came to see her from Sussex, and they always seemed to be respectable people.

Patty Sidney, of no stated occupation, told how she had seen Harriet at both the Alhambra and the Casino, often in the company of different men. She knew of no regular companion and did not think men quarrelled over her. She recalled seeing Harriet at the Alhambra on Christmas Eve, drinking with others, but did not know who these people were.

The next witness was Maryon Russell, who had known Harriet for three months. A few days before the murder, Harriet had asked her to read a letter to her from her sister. Harriet had been invited to spend Christmas with her family in Sussex. She declined the invitation without giving Maryon any reason. This was even the case when another letter came, offering to pay her fare if money was a problem.

A startling discovery occurred in late January. The police had been keeping a watch on foreign vessels in Ramsgate harbour. They

Ramsgate harbour, c.1915. The Royal Hotel, where the Hessels stayed, is on the right. Author's collection

became suspicious of a number of Germans who had travelled up to London from Ramsgate on 22 December. Their ship, the *Wangerland*, was carrying a number of German emigrants to Brazil, but had been forced into the harbour. Suspicion fell on Carl Wohlebe, the surgeon's mate, and Dr Hermann Hessel, a young clergyman. Witnesses were brought down to Ramsgate to identify them. Although the former was cleared, the latter was identified as the man seen with the victim before she was killed. He was arrested and brought to London.

Meanwhile, another man gave himself up for the murder. This was one John King. The police summoned their witnesses to see if they could identify him. King was placed in a room with forty to fifty others, and the witnesses entered one by one to see if they could pick him out. None could. Though aged thirty, he did not resemble the killer in any other way. Although drunk when he first made the confession, he persisted in it when sober. The police held him for a few days before releasing him.

On 29 January, proceedings against Hessel began at the Bow Street Magistrates' Court. However, doubts quickly emerged. Of the three witnesses who identified him, one said that the killer was somewhat taller than the accused man. Yet another witness said Hessel was not the man. However, there was other evidence against him. The hotelier told that Hessel, on his return to the Royal Hotel, Ramsgate, had asked for turpentine to rid his clothes of paint and that his laundry included several handkerchiefs stained with blood – indeed one of them was saturated. A number of witnesses from the hotel spoke in detail about this evidence and the movements of Hessel in December and January.

Other witnesses talked about Harriet's last movements. She had dined at the Hotel Cavour with a man. He had had a dark grey coat, velvet collar and an alpine hat and was a foreigner and was probably middle class – above the rank of a mechanic, but below that of a gentleman. They had then been to the Alhambra and travelled back by omnibus. The man had looked down whilst travelling and did not speak.

Meanwhile, at the inquest, witnesses were questioned again over the identification of Hessel. William Stalker, the waiter at the Cavour, was convinced he had correctly identified the man. The barmaid at the Alhambra was less certain, saying Harriet's companion was taller. Fleck was also certain, but his assistants who had been in the shop with him were not positive. Finally, Mary Neston thought Hessel was the man. After all, they had only seen the man briefly and often in poor light, and were probably determined to see someone brought to justice for the murder. They may have been influenced in what they said by press accounts of the murder. Perhaps one or two were influenced by the reward of £200 for the murderer's conviction. There were, therefore, more doubts beginning to emerge over whether Hessel was the murderer.

The second and final day of the hearing at the magistrates' court was 30 January. It was to prove conclusive. It was said that the killer was probably motivated by revenge and had known Harriet for some time. It was argued that Harriet's killer had been sullen whilst with her on the omnibus and in the fruit shop. A man who had just met a woman would be more likely to be talkative and attentive to her. When they arrived at her lodgings, the man hastened up the steps to her room on the second floor in advance of the woman. He evidently knew where her room was.

Hessel did not, therefore, seem to be a likely murderer. Why should he kill a woman with whom he cannot have had any prior acquaintanceship? He had been born in Prussia, had taken his doctorate and then became a clergyman at Danzig. He married in 1872 and served in particular the needs of sailors. He was elected to become the chaplain for a group of German colonists en route to Brazil. Yet his defence did not rest on Hessel's educational or spiritual eminence.

It relied on rather more solid evidence and witnesses who proved he could not have committed the murder whilst he was staying in a

London hotel in late December 1872. It was on the evening of 22 December that Hessel's party arrived in London and stayed at Kroll's Hotel. On the following day, Hessel was ill. On the night of the murder, Wohlebe recalled seeing Hessel in the hotel dining room (10 pm). The porter corroborated the story and attested that Hessel had not left the hotel between 23 and 26 December. A waiter recalled seeing Hessel on several occasions that evening. Peter Kroll, the hotel's proprietor, said he saw Hessel at 11.00 on Christmas Eve. On 28 December they returned to Ramsgate.

Mr Vaughan, the magistrate, said:

> ... it had been conclusively shown that Dr Hessel was not the companion of Harriet Burswell on the night of the murder. The evidence of the witnesses for the prosecution examined at this court undoubtedly pointed at first to Dr Hessel and justified the police in acting as they had done.

Hessel was loudly cheered as he left the courtroom, a free man. Although he was recompensed for his week in custody, some thought he had been badly treated and humiliated. Hessel received a written apology from none other than William Gladstone, then Prime Minister. A public subscription raised £1,000 for the wronged clergyman. The police were seen as being incompetent and responsible for an act of injustice upon an innocent man. The *Daily Telegraph* was caustic:

> The public will learn with satisfaction that a step has actually been taken towards the detection of the Coram Street murder. The step though small, is certain. It is now been conclusively shown, by an indisputable chain of evidence, that, whoever murdered the woman Buswell, it was not Dr Hessel.

Yet one later theorist thought that he was guilty and that the jury had been taken in by the fact that he was an apparently respectable clergyman and a German at that (there not being that prejudice against Germans which had existed and was to recur in the early twentieth century). She thought that his alibi had been concocted from his movements of the previous day and that he was motivated by 'blood-lust'. It is possible that a clergyman might have a strong animus against prostitutes, perhaps especially one who dealt with sailors as the latter are particularly prone to such temptation. Hence he felt driven by religious and moral urges to kill prostitutes. Like all theories, it is possible, but highly unlikely. Would the real killer give bloody linen to be washed, but rather destroy it, by burning or other means? It also seemed that the killer knew his victim reasonably well, walking up the stairs to her room in advance of her and being

William Gladstone, Prime Minister, who wrote a letter of apology to Hessel. John Coulter's collection

untalkative. Hessel could not possibly have known her hitherto as he had only just arrived in London. He was thirty-one, but it is a pity that his appearance were not described, for then they could be matched against Mary Neston's description.

Investigation was made into Hessel's character, and it was found to be dubious. William White, British Consul in Danzig wrote 'It has been even hinted to me that he has been seen by some natives of

Danzig in ... very low company ... but I mention this with the greatest possible reserve'. Apparently Hessel had taught at a private school, but had had to resign in the autumn of 1871 due to financial irregularities. The Hessels had had serious money problems due to their profligate lifestyle and left debts behind them on their way to Brazil. After all, only desperation would lead them to emigrate. Even so, despite all this, there is no hint that Hessel was a man of violence or was the murderer of Harriet.

Waldemar Peacock was an amateur criminologist and had a pamphlet published in about January 1873, where he discussed the crime. Like many amateur sleuths, he was contemptuous of the police and laid out his own suggestions. He thought that the killer had some anatomical knowledge, knowing exactly how to kill her quickly, and was not the man who had dined with Harriet. Instead, he had picked her up on Russell Square as Harriet listened to carol singers. He thought that the man was a paid assassin in the employ of another man, and was not known to Harriet personally, and that the motive was not robbery. He would not be more explicit because he said that this would put the criminal on his guard and thought that Harriet's correspondence would give the police a clue, though he also wrote 'The police as detectives are palpably inefficient'.

Other suspects were questioned; including a member of a troop of Japanese jugglers and a fellow of the Society of Antiquaries (because of photograph of jugglers and a letter from the Society of Antiquaries being found in Harriet's room), but the killer was never found. The police had put all their trust in eyewitness identification, which was to prove very unreliable. Having no other credible suspect, they fixed on Hessel to the exclusion of anyone else, a not uncommon policy. Why was Harriet killed? Was money the motive or was it an act of revenge or passion? Or was it a case of blackmail? Harriet had talked of better things in the future, though this may have been only what she hoped might happen. Clearly Harriet trusted the man and probably knew him from previous encounters. We shall never know the truth. In all probability as soon as the man left the house there was very little chance of his ever being apprehended.

CHAPTER 12

The Thames Trunk Murder 1873

The body has not been dissected for anatomical purposes, but has been cut up immediately after death.

The River Thames is crucial to London's story. On a grim note, it is also a favoured place to dispose of bodies. We have already noted one such attempt, which occurred on Waterloo Bridge in 1857. The one chronicled here is, if anything, even more gruesome and revolting.

On Friday morning, 5 September 1873, Richard Fane, of the Thames Police, along with two of his colleagues, were on patrol in their boat. Fane later recalled the scene:

> *We were rowing up the river towards Chelsea Bridge, having come from Somerset House. About 6.30 am we were opposite the Battersea Water-works, and off the Surrey shore. The tide was then very near low water. I observed something on the shore, about three or four yards from the water. I put the boat ashore and told one of my brother officers to get out and see what it was. He went to it, and then called me to come and see it. I saw that it was a portion of a woman's body, being the left breast [actually the left portion of a female trunk] entire.*

Fane took the piece to his superiors, who directed him to take it to the parish in which it was found. He went to Battersea and the divisional surgeon, Dr Kempster, then examined it. Kempster's initial report ran as follows:

> *I have examined at the Battersea Police Station the left quarter of the thorax of a woman of fair skin and somewhat fat. Death has taken place within a few hours. The head, arm and other side of the thorax and rest of the body have been separated by a knife and saw, and that in an unscientific manner. The body has not been dissected for anatomical purposes, but has been cut up immediately after death. The vessels are quite empty.*

As time went by, more discoveries were made. The police made a thorough search of the banks of the Thames. A policeman in the

The Wrench Series, No. 3652

Chelsea Bridge, c.1900. Part of the corpse was found near here. Author's collection

employ of the railways found the right portion of the trunk off Brunswick Wharf near to the Nine Elms Station. Inspector Marley of the Thames Police found part of the lungs under an arch of old Battersea Bridge and the remainder near Battersea railway pier. On the following day, parts of the face were found off Limehouse. All these remains were brought together at the Wandsworth Workhouse.

Kempster made a fresh report based on these new finds:

I have examined the scalp and portion of the skin of the face of a woman, aged presumably about forty. The integuement has been separated from the bone with a sharp instrument, and was cut irregularly in several places. The head was covered with short dark hair, very thin, the eyebrows are dark, and there is a very thin dark moustache. The ears are somewhat coarse and pierced for earrings, which have not, however, been torn out. The end of the nose has been severed from the root and is attached to a portion of the upper lip. It is short, thick and round at the extremity. There is a large bruise on the right temple, which was caused by a blow from a blunt instrument or substance shortly before death. The scalp was divided at the upper margin of the bones, but I cannot determine whether before or after death.

On 8 September, more body parts were discovered. The right thigh was found just off Woolwich and the right shoulder near Greenwich. The latter was smeared with tar. It was noted that the heavier parts of the body had probably been deposited not far from where the Wandle enters the Thames and washed down with the tide, unless they were dropped off piece by piece, along the Thames. On the next day, a left forearm was located off the Albert Bridge in Battersea. The other thigh was found, as was the lower part of the trunk. A foot and a forearm were found on 10 September off Lambeth and Rotherhithe.

Enquiries were made as to the identity of the unfortunate middle-aged woman. A partial description of the woman was published in the press. She was about forty, with dark and very thin hair, which had been cut short. She may have recently been suffering from an illness or had been in prison. There was a scar on the left breast, probably caused by an old burn.

Many people called at the workhouse to see whether the remains were of someone known to them. A Bermondsey man was convinced that it was his daughter, one Eliza Wood, but since the victim had not been suffering from small pox as his daughter was, it could not have been her. In fact, his daughter was later seen in Waterloo Road. A sixty-year-old man from Hoxton thought it might be his thirty-nine-year-old daughter, who had been missing for three weeks. He said that his son-in-law had had to bury his mother and he left his wife in London. She had taken to drink. In some respects the remains were similar to his daughter – being almost bald on the top of her head and

The Thames from Tower Bridge, c.1905. In 1873, parts of an unknown woman's corpse were found along the river. Author's collection

London from Tower Bridge   Valentines Series   20853

with very dark hair and wearing earrings. But it was less certain as to other features whether the dead woman had been his daughter. One theory was that the woman was Dutch, and was associated with a Dutch vessel on the Thames.

Another possibility was put forward by Mrs Christian, a Battersea landlady. One of her female lodgers, one Mary Ann Cailey, had been missing since 2 September. She thought that the description matched. Her lodger had been recently left by her husband and was paying 20 shillings a week in rent. Although she had no spare clothes where she lodged, she talked about having great expectations. Apparently the woman often returned home late at night and had been attacked by a gang of four men while travelling over Victoria Bridge in the early morning a few weeks before.

Mrs Christian and her other lodger, one Mrs Lawson, went to see the remains which had been fitted up on a dummy so as to resemble the woman when alive, as far as was possible. This had not been done in the similar case in 1857. They made a positive identification. So did the policeman who had interviewed her after she reported her earlier and non-fatal assault.

The inquest began at the workhouse on 8 September. The policemen, including Fane, who had found various parts of the body gave their evidence about how they had made their discoveries and what they had done with the evidence. Dr Kempster then explained how he had been called in to investigate and what he had found. He concentrated on anatomical details. He thought that the woman was stout, but perfectly healthy. She had once been pregnant. He also noted that on the right temple there was a large bruise, probably caused just before death.

The inquest was resumed a week later. Again, the men who had subsequently found parts of the body spoke about their discoveries. Dr Kempster told the court about what the remains of the body suggested. She had been hit on the head shortly before death, but whether this blow killed her was unclear. There was a small scar near the elbow and another near the knee. A saw and a knife would have been needed to cut up the corpse, and this occurred shortly after death. This would have been a hard manual task if only one man was involved, but it was still possible.

Then there was some more discussion as to the identity of the dead woman. Mrs Cailey's brother declared that he did not think the corpse was that of his sister. Mrs Christian elaborated on the subject of her recent lodger. She had stayed with her since early August, having come from Dorsetshire in order to settle her affairs. She was five feet eight inches in height and was stout. She had left the house at 10.00 am on the morning of 2 September; three days before the first remains of the body were found. Mrs Cailey had told her landlady that she was going out to a pawnshop to retrieve her goods and then to see a solicitor in order to obtain money owing to her. Mrs Christian added that her lodger often returned very late at night, but was never drunk and never had guests. The final verdict was that the deceased, whoever she was, had been murdered by person or persons unknown.

Another theory was that a bargeman's wife, one Mrs Bignell, was missing, presumed dead. A detective went in pursuit of a suspect in line with this theory – a bargeman had been heard shortly before the murder quarrelling with his wife and threatening to kill her. The barge, *The Ann* was traced to Higham, near Rochester, before moving to Crawford and then to Gravesend. But the pursuit was fruitless. The detective met the bargeman's wife.

As with the Waterloo Bridge murder of 1857, there was a suggestion that the body being cut up was the work of medical students. However, medical schools were not open again after the summer holidays until 1 October. Furthermore, it would have been difficult to remove a corpse from the dissecting room in any case, and the cuts on the body were not done by someone with any knowledge of anatomy or surgery. Hospitals and schools of medicine had been checked, but none reported that a corpse was missing.

It was remarked upon that although most of the corpse was eventually found, over a number of days, no trace of any clothing was found. This must have been disposed of separately. If it had not been burnt or buried, it may have been discarded into or near the Thames. Many people scavenged what they could from the Thames and sold it to low-class shopkeepers. Perhaps the dead woman's clothing had been found by someone and sold for a few pence, rather than be handed over to the police who would not pay for it. A valuable clue may have been lost in this manner.

There were no clues to follow up, nor suspects to question. In desperation, on 16 September, the authorities offered a reward of £200 to anyone who could identify the killer. The killer's accomplice, if he had one, would receive a free pardon if he told the police about his associate. Meanwhile, the police had the remains photographed, but would not release a copy of the picture for general viewing, closing off what might have been a fruitful line of enquiry. The Thames was dredged in order to find any more clues. None were.

Finally, the identity of the victim was plunged into mystery once more. On 17 September, Mrs Cailey was found alive and well. She had not come forward previously because she had been with a man in Scotland and had only just returned to London. She then had been too agitated to read about the crime in the newspapers.

Two more possibilities were brought to the attention of the police after the discovery of the live Mrs Cailey. The first concerned Thomas Lay of Barnes, who on 1 September at the Boileau Arms in Barnes, near to the Hammersmith Bridge, 'witnessed a disturbance between a man and a woman (travelling chair makers) he saw the man strike the woman several times, she screamed "Murder and Police"'. Enquiries were made, but no one else had heard anything and they 'being persons of a somewhat superior class for the position they occupy, we [the police] have no reason to doubt their statement'.

Another possibility was related in a letter sent in January 1874. One Mr Hackham had seen the picture of the dead woman and noted 'there appears to be a Great Resemblance to the person passing as Mrs Carter'. Mrs and Thomas Carter had lived in a hotel in Salisbury Street, the Strand, and 'they often did not live very happily together, she having often been heard to say that she wished he would fall down stairs and break his neck'. Yet he was not certain that Mrs Carter was the woman who died, because of his uncertainty as to dates. It is unknown whether the police followed up this line of enquiry.

What had happened was, in one way, straightforward. A woman had been killed on the night of 4 September, perhaps by a blow to the head. The killer, probably a strong man, had chopped up the body and then thrown the remains into the Thames, probably near Battersea. The dismemberment was almost certainly in order to conceal his victim's identity because there was an obvious link to him otherwise. The victim may have been the killer's wife or lover. He probably stripped the clothing from her before setting about his revolting task and disposed of that elsewhere. Had the clothing been found, a clue might have been brought to light, but it never was. With no clue as to her identity, his was equally unknown, as was the motive.

The Times noted:

> It is not pleasant to reflect that, in our high civilization, any one, however poor or friendless, can thus be made away with; but it is inevitable that the art of detection should remain somewhat in the wake of crime, and that the best efforts of the police should be sometimes baffled by the union of vulpine cunning with unscrupulous brutality.

Regrettably it was not the last of such crimes – less than a year later, a trunk of a woman was found in the Thames off Putney. Was there any connection? This murder, too, remained unsolved.

CHAPTER 13

The Smell in the Cellar
1880

*I cannot give any explanation of this
mystery of the cask with the body
under the cistern in the inner cellar.*

ohn Spendlove, butler to Mr Jacob Henriques of Harley
Street, had noticed a smell coming from the cellar of his
master's house for some time. Indeed, it had been notice-
able ever since he had begun to work there in November 1878. Arthur
Kirkland, the footman, had also detected it, but had not thought
much more about it. It did not emanate from the dustbin, nor did it
seem to be from the large cask which contained bottles, pushed under
the cistern and blocked from view by a champagne case. Perhaps it
was the drains? Spendlove communicated this thought to Henriques,
who had workmen in to examine them, but still the odour remained.

On Thursday morning of 3 June 1880, Spendlove decided to investigate the cask more closely. Taking out the bottles, he saw something which looked like an effigy in the dim light of the cellar. He
called Kirkland and between them they dragged the mummified effigy
from the cask, before realizing what it was. It was the remains of a
human corpse.

Spendlove interrupted his master's breakfast with the grim news.
He told the butler to fetch the police. Spendlove delegated the task
to Kirkland and two constables arrived. The body was removed to
Marylebone Workhouse, where it was examined by doctors Bond and
Spurgin.

The corpse was very much decomposed and had been covered in
quicklime. Had chloride of lime been used instead, the body would
have been wholly destroyed. The body was that of a middle-aged
woman of poor circumstances, perhaps aged between forty and fifty
years. She had dark brown hair and was short.

Meanwhile, Chief Inspector Stephen Lucas led the investigation.
The cellar was searched for clues. Little was found except a few scraps
of underclothing which had belonged to the corpse. It was also learnt
that the cellar was kept unlocked, so anyone could have entered it.

No one in the house could shed any light on the corpse. Henriques had lived there since the 1850s. He was a sixty-eight-year-old retired merchant, and had been born in Jamaica. He and his family of four had a holiday for a month or six weeks every autumn. He cooperated with the police and gave them a list of all the servants (in 1881 they had seven) he had employed in the preceding three years. One Henry Smith had been his butler prior to Spendlove.

The inquest was held on 7 June at Marylebone. Dr Hardwicke, the coroner for central Middlesex, presided. First, the jury were taken to view the remains of the corpse. Then Spendlove explained that he usually slept on the premises and his room was near the cellar, unless he was with his wife in Wimbledon.

Mr Spurgin, the police surgeon, gave the bulk of the evidence submitted to the jury. He told how he examined the corpse. There were remains of stockings and garters adhering to the legs. Otherwise the body was naked and in an advanced state of decomposition. On the head were a few strands of hair. There was also a red coral bead, once part of a necklace, though no earrings or rings were found. The body was about four feet seven inches in height.

The coroner asked Spurgin how long the body had been decomposing. He thought death had occurred at least a year before, possibly longer. Perhaps it had been there for two years as a maximum. Spurgin also told that he and Dr Pepper had examined the body and found an opening between the fourth and fifth ribs. They found evidence of blood there, too. This was probably the result of her being stabbed, but Spurgin would not commit himself to make any definite statement. Dr Pepper differed from Spurgin and thought the woman's height was four feet ten inches. He also said that the woman might have been only thirty, but not more than her early forties. Death had occurred between eighteen months to two and a half years before. The wound could not have been self-inflicted and was probably caused by a table knife.

The inquest was adjourned until 11 July. Spurgin felt able to commit himself to the cause of death. He said:

> I have examined the body further and more particularly to ascertain the immediate cause of death. I have no doubt that death was caused in this case by a stab in the left breast between the fourth and fifth ribs. There was no appearance of injury to the heart, and as the lung has entirely disappeared the injury to that could not be traced; but the effusion of blood in the region of the stab was abundantly clear, while the right side was free from any such indications.

He added that, before the body had been put into the barrel, it had been either buried in lime or had had this sprinkled upon it. He reached this conclusion because the whole of the body was evenly covered in lime, and there was none on or in the barrel itself. Stains of lime were also found on the remnants of clothing, which were made of coarse materials. There were also bloodstains and smears on the barrel, but these were probably the result of blood coming from the nose or mouth after death. He added that in the cellar there were found a table knife, two old pokers and some rope. The knife was rusty and Spurgin thought that no conclusion could be drawn from that. Such a knife might have been the murder weapon, but after such a time there was no effective test for bloodstains. Finally, he thought it certain that the corpse had been forced into the cask because of the curvature of the spine.

Apart from the medical evidence, the police had found a number of witnesses. The first was Henry Smith, Henriques's butler prior to Spendlove. He was now a soldier in the 3rd Surrey Regiment and separated from his wife. He was as mystified as everybody else, stating at the outset, 'I cannot give any explanation of this mystery of the cask with the body under the cistern in the inner cellar.' He did not recall how it got there in the first place.

Yet it would have been easy for any outsider to have placed it there. Smith had been responsible as butler for locking the gate to the property each night, but said that he did not always do so. There had

Harley Street. The body of an unknown woman was found in the cellar of a rich merchant's house in this street. John Coulter's collection

been no one admitted to the house surreptitiously, but he had often let William Tinapp, a German and then footman, back in after the latter had been out drinking. In fact, when Henriques had heard of this, Smith was sacked – sometime in the autumn of 1878. He mentioned that he had asked a man to dig a hole in the cellar in order that the stale bread which he had accumulated could be concealed from his master. The hole, though, had never been dug.

The next witness was the would-be hole-digger. This was John Green, an elderly coachman of Weymouth Mews. He recalled being asked by Smith about his abilities as a paviour, and visited the cellar with him. All he did was to put bricks into a small hole in the cellar. He had little knowledge what was in the cellar, except that the knife and pokers were not there. He did not mention the cask.

Tinapp was the next to speak. He had worked for Henriques in 1878. He thought the cask was there when he worked there and that it smelt. He recalled that bricks in the cellar had been removed and then replaced. Mrs Jewry, who had been cook from 1874 to 1879, did not think that there ever had been such a wastage of bread that it would need to be buried, and if there had been, it could have been removed by the dustmen. George Campbell, another former butler, who had worked there for five months in 1877–8, said that he did not recall the cask being in the cellar, nor any odour. John Borthman and George Minton also attested to this fact.

Others were called to give evidence. Mr Woodruff had been the caretaker of the house in 1878 when the family had been away for some weeks, and had undertaken this role for the past six years. He had seen the cask in the cellar in the autumn of 1878, but thought it merely full of bottles. At this time, Smith was with the family in the country and on these occasions the caretaker always locked the gate.

Inspector King had investigated the hole, and told the jury it was once a cess-pit. He also said that, shortly after Smith was fired, a valuable piece of jewellery was missing. There had been a search of the cellar and the bricks had been taken up at that time, too. The jury was unable to put forward any verdict save that an unknown woman had been stabbed to death by a person unknown.

A reward of £100 was offered in order to try and catch the killer, but no one ever tried to claim it. Many letters were sent to the police, offering suggestions as to who the murdered woman was. Further enquiries revealed the whereabouts of these women. But one had evidently vanished without anyone noticing.

One theory was that the corpse was of the wife of a former servant who left him for a post in the country. She returned, but was never seen again. Another possibility was that the corpse was that of Eliza

Varndell, aged about forty, who lived nearby, working as a servant, but became unemployed and she too was never seen again.

What had happened was this. A poor woman had been stabbed to death in the latter half of 1878 and had been covered with lime. She had then been thrust into a cask and placed in Henriques's cellar – an easy task given that Smith often said the gate was unlocked and the cellar could be entered from the outside of the house. The killer was almost certainly a man, probably married, and a strong one to have thrust the corpse into the cask and then to have moved the cask into the cellar. He had access to lime; perhaps he worked with it, and was probably of the same social class and age as his victim. The victim was probably his wife or mistress, certainly someone with whom he could be connected; hence all the trouble he took to try and dispose of the body. The murderer probably lived close by to Harley Street, as it would have been risky to have moved a cask too far. Could Smith have been the killer? The corpse was placed in the cellar during his time of employment there. Perhaps he first tried to dispose of the corpse under the cellar and used the need to bury stale bread as the excuse to employ Green to dig the hole. Yet this is merely a hypothesis as there is no other evidence to identify him as the killer. It could well have been an outsider, but clearly one who knew the house well enough to know the cellar was easily accessible; perhaps by gossip from a servant or a tradesman.

Chapter 14

The West Ham Serial Murders?
1881–1890

... very grave suspicions attached to a certain individual. Legal proofs were wanting, and there was no sufficient evidence to justify an arrest.

everal children went missing from West Ham between 1881 and 1890 (some writers claim there were a dozen, but I have found no evidence of this). Emily Huckle, aged thirteen, but looking sixteen, had been discharged from her job as a servant on 7 February 1881. She was never seen again. The second was Mary Seward, aged fourteen, who left her home in West Road, West Ham, at 6.00 pm on 13 April 1881 to look for her little nephew. Despite the offer of a reward and an appeal in the press, she was never seen again. Nearly a year later, the local paper commented 'Where she is none can say; what wretchedness she has undergone in the interval, who dares guess?'

The third was Eliza Carter, aged twelve, on 28 January 1882. She was living with her sister – again on West Road – and went out in the evening to another house on that road with a bundle of clothes at 10.30 pm. She was later seen at 11.00 pm in Stratford High Street, with a large, heavy set woman, wearing a long ulster coat and a black frock. On the following day, her blue dress was found on the football pitch. All the buttons had been ripped off. Crumbs were found; presumably she had been enticed with biscuits. It was assumed she had been kidnapped, raped and the body buried somewhere, though an extensive search proved fruitless. However, other theories suggested that she had been kidnapped for the purposes of ransom (though her parents were poor) and that she had been forced into prostitution, 'abducted by wretches who wanted them for purposes of which we can only guess'. There was the suggestion that a reward should be offered for her return, assuming she was still alive.

West Ham Park, c.1900. In 1882, clothing belonging to the missing girl was found here. Author's collection

Other girls had also been attacked locally in January 1882. One seven year old had been lured to a remote part of the park by a man who sexually assaulted her. Another girl had been offered inducements to accompany a man, but had refused. A young female servant of the vicar, Canon Thomas Scott (1831–1914) was attacked by a 'ruffianly fellow', but managed to fight off her attacker. There was criticism in the local press about the lack of adequate policing.

Charles Wagner, a butcher's son, was the next victim on 2 April 1882, but his case was different. First, he was a seventeen-year-old lad and, second, the motive for his murder – he was found at the foot of the cliffs at Ramsgate – was almost certainly robbery as he was taking his father's takings, amounting to £150, to the bank. One James Walters, an older employee of his father's, was accused of the crime and was given seven years in prison. He was definitely guilty of theft and probably of murder, too. It is possible that Walters and Wagner worked together and later fell out. His death may have no connection with the other disappearances.

Hannah Evans, a sixteen-year-old servant, was sent on an errand on the evening of 27 November 1882. She worked in a house on King's Road, Upton Park. Once again, that was the last time anyone recorded seeing her.

It is worth noting that West Ham grew at an enormous rate in the final decades of the nineteenth century. Population soared, from 128,953 in 1881 to 204,893 in 1891, as did the rate at which new housing was erected. The latter meant that it was probably easier to conceal corpses as land was being covered with housing. It also meant that many newcomers were coming into the district – a few, perhaps, with sinister intent.

Of course it is possible that these girls all gravitated to the centre of London or elsewhere. Most of those who disappear are young women, often leaving because of alleged parental domination or trouble at home, and lured by the 'bright lights' of the city. All too often, however, they fall prey to prostitution and pornography. They were not necessarily all victims of a killer. Yet an examination of the 1891 census index does not reveal that any of these young women were alive then, although it is possible they changed their names or emigrated. But they may all have been murdered.

There is no doubt about the final victim. Unlike the others, she was found, but not alive. She was Amelia Jeffs, who was fifteen years old and lived with her parents, Charles, a railway employee (Eliza Carter's father worked for the railways, too), and Mary, in a house on West Road (the same street as Eliza and Mary). She was tall for her age, with blue eyes, fair hair, a fresh complexion and was good looking. She attended Canon Scott's local school (presumably the National School on Church Road North). Scott was also a school-master. Amelia was employed by a Mrs Harvey in an unknown capacity, though presumably as a servant.

She was last seen alive on the afternoon of Friday 31 January 1890. George Gardiner, a thirteen year old, said that he saw Amelia walking slowly along Stanley Terrace in the direction of the church, carrying a basket. The time was between about 6.30 and 6.45 pm. Then she was seen by a girl called Harmer in West Street, who thought she was waiting for someone. When George returned he did not see Amelia in West Street.

Amelia's mother was ill, so her daughter was sent out on an errand. Amelia left home at 6.30 pm to go to the fish and chip shop, three-quarters of a mile away. She set out with 3 pence, a latch key and a basket. She never reached the shop and did not return home. Mr and Mrs Jeffs began to worry at about 7.30 pm.

Her father went to the West Ham Police Station and reported his daughter's disappearance. Inspector James Harvey gave the following order to his men:

> *Very special attention of all ranks is drawn to the disappearance of Amelia Jeffs from her house, 38 West Road. All houses, out-houses, &c., to which the police have access, to be carefully examined to see if she can be found therein. No effort on our part should be spared to trace the girl, whose disappearance is mysterious.*

Despite searches made by the police, including searches of coffee houses and lodging houses, no trace of the girl could be found. On

Portway, West Ham, c.1920s. The corpse of Amelia Jeffs was found in a house here in 1890. Author's collection

10 February 1890, Canon Scott wrote to *The Times* to voice his concerns and to issue an appeal in order to locate her. He also noted that some years ago, two other girls had gone missing.

However, four days later, a grim discovery was made. Joseph Roberts, a thirteen year old, entered one of the empty houses in Portway, a street in West Ham connected with West Road, by the back window, which was open, looking for empty lemonade bottles. There was a peculiar odour from one of the rooms. He told his father, who told him to tell the police. Sergeant Forth went to investigate on the following day. He made a thorough search of the property. Nothing could be found on the ground floor which would account for the odour. However, in the attic there was found a cupboard, which was locked and seemed to conceal the source of the smell. According to a newspaper:

> *The door was forced, and a horrible sight met the eyes of the constables, the body of a decaying girl being discovered lying on the floor. The body was in a partial state of decomposition, and upon its being taken from the cupboard it was found that a piece of rope had been drawn tightly round the neck, causing strangulation.*

Amelia had been found. The girl had been brutally thrust into the cupboard with great violence and had also been 'outraged' (raped).

An ambulance and the police doctor were sent for, and the corpse was conveyed to the local mortuary. In the cupboard were the basket and the latch key.

More was found out about the unlet house in which the corpse had been found. It, along with seven others, had been built about a year before, but tenants could not be found for them. A watchman called Joseph Roberts kept them under some form of supervision. All the doors were locked and the windows fastened. No one was known to have gone inside any for three months. At the back of the houses was a large field (now West Ham Park), but a wooden fence separated this from the houses.

The inquest was concluded in early March at the King's Head Tavern on Church Street. Roberts recalled that he, in the company of some policemen, had entered some of the houses in November of the previous year, as lead had been stolen from some of the properties. He also said that he had not got a key for the house in which the body was found (it had been missing for some time) and did not think they had entered that property in November.

Joseph Hotton was the carpenter employed by Roberts to fit locks to the houses, which he had done in March 1889. He said there were two keys to each house. Roberts had been given one for each and the others were placed in the cupboards of storerooms of each.

Dr Grogono gave the medical evidence. He had examined the corpse on 1 March, two weeks after its discovery. He found bloodstains on the flannel petticoat, the chemise and the underflannel. He did not think the girl's scarf was used to strangle her, though strangulation had been the cause of death. He thought that she had been unconscious when she was assaulted, but could not be sure. Presumably this meant that there had been no signs of any struggle, though one report mentions bruising to the limbs, which suggests a struggle did occur.

After hearing all the evidence, the coroner summed up. He added that the police had been inundated with letters from all over the country, most of which were anonymous. He seemed to believe that entry to the house had been by the front, and the criminal must have had a key to the door, due to the girl's footprint being found in the dust. The two probably knew each other, as it seemed they had conversed in the house for a time. He then postulated that she was raped and then killed in order to stop the vicious perpetrator being identified. The jury found that Amelia had been killed by person or persons unknown.

Amelia's funeral attracted a large crowd, as was usual for those of murder victims, especially those who were killed in such atrocious circumstances. Scott performed the service and hoped that God

Parish Church, West Ham, c.1900. The vicar, the Revd Scott, preached at Amelia's funeral service here. Author's collection

would forgive the killer, but also that he be brought to earthly justice. The feelings of the mourners were similar – one wreath reading 'Vengeance is mine, I will repay, saith the Lord'. Funeral expenses were defrayed by an anonymous man, and the reward for the capture of her killer exceeded £100, all subscribed by well wishers.

In May, the missing keys were found in a crack in the brick wall in the attic of the house where the murder had been committed. It was assumed that the killer must have recently replaced them there.

Sir Melville Macnaghten confessed that the police were unable to solve this crime. However, he hinted that the killer was not unknown to them, writing, 'in the latter, very grave suspicions attached to a certain individual. Legal proofs were wanting, and there was no sufficient evidence to justify an arrest, it must be classified as an "undiscovered [i.e. unsolved] crime"'. Macnaghten was famously discreet in not revealing information about murderers in unsolved crimes – although he claimed to have 'private information' about Montague Druitt being the Ripper, he withheld it even in a confidential memorandum. A newspaper report made a similar assertion, 'the evidence against the author of the crime was deemed insufficient to justify his arrest ... popular suspicion did grave injustice to an innocent man'. So we are as much in the dark as we were before he made his teasing non-revelation.

Were the disappearances of the other girls connected to that of Amelia Jeffs? It seems possible that they were all the victims of the same man who had a perverse penchant for young girls, all of whom had lived in West Road or not far away. He had skilfully hidden the remains of all of them, but had been less fortunate with the last (perhaps he meant to conceal the body in a better place but the corpse was found before he was able to do so). Somehow he must have lured the unfortunate girls to somewhere where he could molest them, and may have appeared quite respectable if he was a stranger, unless he was a local man well known to them and so trusted. The latter seems more likely, however. He may have been a neighbour or friend of the family, or a figure of authority, such as a teacher, clergyman, police-man or doctor. But why did he wait nearly eight years between victims before striking again? Could it have been because he was in prison? Could Walters, the probable killer of Wagner, be responsible, as he was in gaol between 1882 and 1889? Yet his one probable murder was of a young man and the motive was robbery, not rape, and he was in gaol when Hannah disappeared. It is not known if Roberts was sus-pected, as he had a key, though it had been allegedly lost. He certainly might have been the killer as he was resident in West Ham from at least 1881. Or had the man who stole the key used it? Or had Hotton made three keys, not declared the third and kept it to be used as part of a vile scheme? Hotton was not resident in West Ham in 1881, so, assuming the same man killed all three girls, he must be excluded.

One suspect is Canon Scott himself. He had been vicar of the parish church of All Saints, West Ham, since 1867 and was to leave the parish in the year after Amelia's death, to go to Lavenham in Suffolk, as rector. Furthermore, he lived with his family in the vicarage on Portway. He was in the right place at the right times and probably knew, and was trusted by, all the girls as both their schoolmaster and their clergyman. It is not uncommon for paedophiles to be married and have large families, as Scott had. Was he Macnaghten's suspect? Or was he the innocent man wrongly suspected? Yet if he was the killer, why did he draw attention to the disappearances in *The Times*? His departure to Lavenham may be a coincidence and might have been caused by his horror of the murders or because he was falsely accused, as some man certainly was. Furthermore, if he was the killer, why did he not operate between 1882 and 1890, for he was certainly in West Ham, as proved by directories and letters written by him? He might have been the killer, but just as easily might not. There were no reports of similar outrages in Lavenham. Finally, two young girls, Florence Ralph and Bertha Russ, were killed in West Ham in 1895 and 1899, respectively, and their killer never found – could they have been other victims of the same man? If so, Scott is definitely ruled out.

In August 1892, a twenty-three-year-old labourer from Walthamstow confessed to having poisoned Amelia. Yet, on investigation, it was found that he was in prison at the time of the murder and had previously been in an asylum on two occasions. He later confessed to another murder of a young girl. His name was George Bush.

The murder of Amelia Jeffs was a premeditated and cowardly crime – the criminal had probably already committed similar crimes. A foul deed – fouler, perhaps, by the fact that the murderer was never brought to justice.

Chapter 15

Jack the Ripper's Final Victims? (1)
1889

... the murderer, who, I am inclined to believed is identical with the notorious 'Jack the Ripper' of last year.

It would be impossible to write a book about unsolved Victorian murders and to omit the most infamous killer of them all – the man dubbed 'Jack the Ripper'. Many of the books about Britain's most infamous murderer, and all the films and television dramas about him, assume there were five murders committed by this unknown man in London's East End in the autumn of 1888. These were Mary Nichols (31 August), Annie Chapman (8 September), Elizabeth Stride and Catherine Eddowes (30 September) and Mary Jane Kelly (9 November). The victims were all prostitutes of Whitechapel and Spitalfields. All had had their throats cut and, save Elizabeth Stride (who some believe was not a Ripper victim), all were shockingly mutilated. All, save Mary Kelly, were middle aged. No one was ever convicted for these crimes.

Despite the many books about the Ripper and the numerous solutions offered, his identity remains unknown. Witness statements about men seen with the victims vary considerably. He was probably a local man, with great knowledge of the streets and alley ways of the East End. He was probably young – in his twenties and thirties and reasonably strong. He was probably single and in regular employment, right-handed and had a degree of anatomical knowledge. He may have been British or may have been a foreigner. He was probably a loner and was certainly psychologically disturbed, probably from childhood. The motive for the murders was probably a hatred of women in general and prostitutes in particular, driven by sadistic impulses.

There was no single police view as to who the Ripper was. Inspector Frederick Abberline, a principal officer in the case, thought that George Chapman, a serial poisoner, was guilty and when he was arrested in 1903 declared, 'You've got Jack the Ripper at last!' Yet Sir Robert Anderson, Assistant Commissioner of the CID, and Chief Inspector Donald Swanson, thought the criminal was a Polish Jew. This may have been one Aaron Kosminski or David Cohen. Sir Melville Macnaghten, Assistant Chief Constable, opted for three suspects; the aforementioned Kosminski, Montague John Druitt, a barrister who committed suicide a month after Mary Kelly's death, and Michael Ostrog, a Russian con man and thief. Chief Inspector John Littlechild, head of Special Branch, confided to a journalist in 1913 that one Francis Tumblety, an American homosexual quack doctor and a petty thief, was perhaps the killer. Basil Thomson confused suspects and claimed 'in the belief of the police he was a man who committed suicide in the Thames at the end of 1888' (which sounds like Druitt) but also wrote that this man was an insane Russian doctor (which sounds like Ostrog). Yet there are good reasons for doubting that any of these men were the Ripper. No police file exists about any of them, suggesting that the police were very far from certain about their chosen suspects.

Many of the theories about his identity hinge on there being five victims and in this year. The men (Montague John Druitt and Sir William Gull, an elderly royal physician) accused, respectively, by Daniel Farson in *Jack the Ripper* and by Stephen Knight in *The Final Solution* and the films, were dead by 1890, though there are good reasons to indicate that these two men were entirely innocent of mass murder. Another suspect, James Maybrick, a Liverpool businessman, died in 1889. More recently, authors have suggested that perhaps at least eight women were killed by the same man, beginning with Martha Tabram on 7 August 1888 and concluding with the two to be described in this chapter and the next (who were killed in 1889 and 1891). If the latter two killings were Ripper murders, then some of the men mentioned are completely innocent, without any doubt (Tumblety and Chapman were in America, Druitt, Gull and Maybrick were dead and, by the time of the 'last' murder, Kosminski was in an asylum). Of course it is possible that the later killings were copycat murders committed by someone entirely different and so we are back to square one.

Rather than produce yet another account of the murders, much of which is very familiar, I have decided to concentrate on what may – or may not – have been the last two murders, as these are least known to many. Books about the murders written by Donald Rumbelow, Paul Begg and Philip Sugden can be recommended to anyone requiring detailed accounts of the whole series of killings, as they concentrate on facts, not theories. As Sugden rightly observes, many authors select a suspect as killer and choose their evidence to 'prove' it, ignoring that which does not suit them.

In the summer of 1889, the East End appeared to be a slightly less dangerous place. There had been no 'Ripper' killings since 9 November 1888. Scotland Yard still received letters about the mysterious killer, or some alleging to be from the murderer. One of the latter read that he was 'to resume operations in July'. Although this was probably from a crank or a hoaxer, it came true.

Police Sergeant Badham wrote, rather ungrammatically, in his report on 17 July:

> *I beg to report that about 12.48 am 17th inst. I visited PC272H Walter Andrews in Castle Alley, Whitechapel. He being on Beat No. 11 on the 4th Section. I said to him alright he replied alright Sergeant. I then left him and went to visit another P.C. on an adjoining beat. I had only got about 150 yards from P.C. 272H when I heard a whistle blown twice. I rushed to the bottom of Castle Alley and heard P.C. 272H say come on quick he ran up the alley, and I followed, and on the pavement closer to two vans on the right hand side of the footpath I saw a woman laying on her right side with her clothes half way up her waist exposing her abdomen. I also noticed a quantity of blood under her head on the footway. The P.C. said here's another murder . . .*

The body was warm and more police were summoned in order to try and find any 'suspicious looking' men seen lurking about. Detective Inspector Reid examined the corpse, which was lying just under a lamp post. It was of a woman aged about forty, five feet four inches in height, with brown hair and brown eyes, dressed in a red dress. Under her body were an old clay pipe and a farthing. Needless to say, perhaps, her throat had been cut and there were other marks of a knife on her corpse. Dr George Phillips (the divisional police surgeon), who had examined the corpses of all the previous victims, pronounced her dead and the body was taken by ambulance to Whitechapel mortuary. Castle Alley, it is worth noting, was only two streets away from where Martha Tabram's body (stabbed thirty-nine times) had been found in West Street eleven months earlier.

PC Andrews, who had found the body, said he saw no one in the street at the time, but when he blew his whistle to summon aid, he did see one Isaac Jacob, a bootmaker. This man was going to Wentworth Street with his plate in search of his supper. There were a number of wagons and carts along Castle Alley, which were searched, to no avail. Despite a thorough search of the district, including lodging houses and coffee houses, nothing relevant was found and no one could be seen on the streets. As before, the killer had seemingly vanished into thin air.

Superintendent Henry Moore, who had worked on the Ripper murders of 1888, was ordered to take charge. He soon had other facts at his fingertips and these he reported on the day of the murder. John McCormac, a labourer, of Gun Street in Spitalfields, had lived with the deceased, who was identified as Alice McKenzie (known as 'Clay Pipe Alice'), for six or seven years. He had last seen her on the previous day, at 4.00 pm, after he finished work. He had then given her some money (1s 8d) for the rent. According to one report, they may have quarrelled, as he said, 'I had a few words, and that upset her'. He then had a drink, went to sleep, and on waking between 10.00 and 11.00 pm noticed that she had gone out. McCormac knew little of her background, apart from the fact she claimed to be from Peterborough. Unlike the victims of 1888, her background is still a mystery.

Betsy Ryder was the deputy in charge of the lodging house where McCormac and Alice lodged. She said the two were on amicable terms and had lived there for about a year. She said that Alice had left between 8.30 and 9.00 pm. She noticed that the woman had some money in her hand, but did not know how much. This was the cash that McCormac had given her to pay the rent and was almost certainly later spent on alcohol, as Mrs Ryder said 'She was much addicted to drink' and had indeed been drinking earlier that evening. Although the police thought Alice was a prostitute, Mrs Ryder was not certain.

Gun Street, 2006. Alice McKenzie resided in a lodging house here. Author's collection

Some said she was a charwoman for local Jews. It has to be said that, even though she had been living with McCormac, she still could easily have been a prostitute – some of the victims of 1888 had walked the streets and yet had long-term lovers. Others attested that she did walk the streets, though she also earned money by more honest ways, too. Mrs Ryder and McCormac identified Alice at the mortuary on the afternoon of the murder.

The inquest began on the same day at the Working Lads' Institute on Whitechapel Road. Little occurred at the first sitting, except identification of the body and the hearing of the testimonies of the policemen who had first found it.

Two doctors examined the corpse. These were Dr Thomas Bond, who had examined Mary Jane Kelly's corpse in the previous year and Dr Phillips. The knife, a strong sharp one, had been thrust deeply into the neck on the left side and drawn across to the right. A jagged incision, seven inches long, had been made to the chest and there were a few other cuts on the body, but none of the savagery which had been inflicted in the previous year. She had probably had a drink that evening.

Other witnesses came forward. Margaret Franklin said that she had known Alice for fourteen or fifteen years. She had seen her on Tuesday evening, 16 July, at about 11.40 pm – a little less than an hour before the murder – on Brick Lane. She had asked Alice how she was and Alice replied, 'All right I can't stop now'. Perhaps she had an assignation with a client? Earlier that evening, Alice had been seen with a blind boy, George Dixon, in a pub near the Cambridge Music Hall at about 6.50 pm. A man bought her a drink there. Dixon was returned to Gun Street where he lived shortly afterwards.

The murder had been committed between about 12.30 (when a constable last went along the alley) and 12.45 am (it began to rain at 12.45 and the ground beneath the corpse was dry). She had been lying on the ground when she met her death. It was possible that the killer had been disturbed in his work, as the constable who found the corpse noted it was still warm. No one had heard anything, but this was probably because she had been surprised by the first cut to her throat and then was unable to scream because of it.

Unfortunately, there were few clues. Moore wrote, 'I wish to point out that every effort is being made to obtain something tangible in regard to the perpetrator of the crime'. The Chief Commissioner of Police James Munro, who had replaced Sir Charles Warren in November 1888, wrote, 'It will be seen that in spite of ample Police precautions and vigilance the assassin has again succeeded in committing a murder and getting off without leaving the slightest clue to his identity.'

A couple of suspects were rounded up, but neither to any effect. John Mills was arrested on the morning of the murder, but was soon discharged. Another, one William Brodie, aged thirty-three, gave himself up. He confessed to nine killings in Whitechapel, but none troubled his conscience until the last one, which is why he confessed. Yet no blood was found on his clothes. Brodie was a petty thief and the police suspected him of being a lunatic, too. Brodie said that he had caught an infection from an East End prostitute. He claimed he met Alice and offered her a shilling for her services. He said he had then killed her and left when he heard someone arriving on the scene. Arnold concluded, 'He appears of unsound mind and I do not think any reliance can be placed upon his statement.'

It may be no more than coincidence, but the *Police Gazette*, only a few weeks after the murder, put out a wanted notice for Michael Ostrog, who was one of the men suspected by Macnaghten as being the Ripper. It was not stated why he was wanted. In any case, Ostrog was not apprehended until 1891 and was not charged with murder.

Walter Dew, then a junior policeman, but later to gain fame for his capture of Crippen, thought that Alice might have been lured to her death by the killer throwing down a shiny coin to the ground. Thinking it a sovereign, his victim went to pick it up – and then he struck. The coin was the farthing found beneath her. He also related that another woman said that she had been approached by a man that night, but she did not go with him. This man was described as 'a dark foreigner, speaking good English'.

Was this the handiwork of Jack the Ripper? Munro certainly thought so, writing on 17 July, 'I need not say that every effort will be made by the Police to discover the murderer, who, I am inclined to believed is identical with the notorious "Jack the Ripper" of last year.' Dr Bond agreed, writing, 'I am of opinion that the murder was performed by the same person who committed the former series of Whitechapel murders.' He thought that the cuts on the body indicated 'sexual thoughts' and a degree of anatomical knowledge. More officers were drafted into the district as a result of the murder.

Yet the more experienced Dr Phillips thought that the weapon used was a small knife, 'smaller than one used in most of the cases that have come under my observation in these "Whitechapel murders"'. He added, the following, arguably ambiguous remarks:

After careful and long deliberation I cannot satisfy myself on purely anatomical & professional grounds that the Perpetrator of all the 'WhChl. Murders' is the man. I am on contrary impelled to a contrary conclusion. This noting the mode of procedure & the character of the mutilations & judging of motive in connection with the latter. I do not here enter into comparison of the cases neither do I take into account what I admit may be almost conclusive evidence in favour of the one man theory if all the surrounding circumstances & other evidence is considered.

Certainly the injuries, though similar to those of the previous years, were rather different. The mutilation was minimal and Alice's throat had not been cut down as far as the spinal cord. Philips also thought that the wounds were inflicted by a left-handed man – as we have seen, the Ripper was probably right-handed. Sir Robert Anderson later wrote that 'I am here assuming the murder of Alice McKenzie was by another hand ... the chief commissioner investigated the case on the spot and decided it was an ordinary murder and not the work of a sexual maniac'. Dew later wrote, 'I do not think this was a Ripper crime'. Thomson thought the crime was due to the 'law of imitation'.

Dr Forbes Winslow, an amateur criminologist, later wrote, 'the monster laid down his knife in July 1889, after the eight victim'. Convinced the police investigation was incompetent, he set to sleuthing himself. According to him there was a long interval between the murders of Mary Kelly and Alice because the killer had a 'lucid interval' between his bouts of insanity. He claimed that he had met a woman who said she had been approached by a man, though she refused him and later, on the day after the murder, saw him in Finsbury, washing his hands. Forbes published his theories in the press and claimed that the killer, whom he was convinced was 'a homicidal monomaniac of religious views', who was aiming to rid the streets of prostitutes, fled to South Africa, and so the murders ceased. There is no evidence to support Forbes's theories, however.

Wynne Baxter the coroner, summing up the evidence at the inquest, which was concluded on 14 August, gave a balanced assessment:

> *There is great similarity between this and the other class of cases which have happened in this neighbourhood, and if this crime has not been committed by the same person, it is clearly an imitation of the other cases. We have another similarity in the absence of motive. None of the evidence shows that the deceased was at enmity with anyone.*

A vicious murder had been committed, without doubt. It may have been the work of the man who killed four to six women in the previous year. It may have been by a copycat killer. Whoever it was left no clues and was unseen, so escaped detection. One presumes that McCormac was not the killer – murders by husbands or lovers are very common; he does not seem to have had his movements checked by the police. But was the East End free of the Ripper?

CHAPTER 16

Jack the Ripper's Final Victims? (2) 1891

There was great excitement.
Ripper panic was revived. My view
was that this was a false alarm.

Alice McKenzie may not have been the last Ripper victim, if indeed she was one at all. There is one last possible candidate for that dubious accolade. It was on the cold winter's morning of Saturday 13 February 1891. The young PC Thompson of H division had only been in the Metropolitan Police Force for two months. It was his first solo night beat and it was to be a most shocking one. At about 2.15 he was walking along Chamber Street and then planned to go under the railway archway of the Great Eastern Railway, on a thoroughfare known as Swallow's Gardens, in order to reach Royal Mint Street, which was the end of his beat.

According to *The Times*:

On entering the arch he did not hear anything unusual, but on reaching the centre he could distinguish the form of a woman lying in the middle of the roadway, which is only wide enough to permit the passing of one vehicle at a time. He could make out that she was lying on her back with the legs crossed at the feet . . . he saw a terrible spectacle. The throat of the unfortunate woman was severed to the spinal column, and blood was flowing freely from the gaping wound.

The woman was still alive, but only just. Thompson later said that one of her eyelids was still moving.

Just as importantly, the murderer was probably not far away. Thompson heard 'the sounds of retreating footsteps'. He thought these were of a man either walking down Chamber Street or from having left the other side of the archway. However, Thompson stayed with the woman. There was criticism of his actions by some. It was argued that, had he been a more experienced officer, he would have immediately given chase. In not doing so, he had lost the opportunity

Chamber Street, 2006. The corpse of Frances Coles was found here in 1891. Author's collection

of apprehending the killer, or at least, gaining a good description of him which might have allowed him to be caught soon afterwards. Frederick Wensley, later Chief Constable, wrote, 'It is probable that had Thompson been a little more experienced he would have taken up the chase of the fugitive immediately. In all likelihood he would have made a capture which might possibly have solved a great mystery.' Yet such a criticism, tempting as it is – after all, if the killer was the Ripper, it seems incomprehensible that any chance should have been neglected to lay him to heels – police regulations laid down that an officer had to stay with a victim whilst they were still alive, and Thompson was merely following orders.

Instead Thompson blew his whistle for assistance. It was soon answered. Police Sergeant Hyde and PC Hinton joined their colleague. Although other police officers arrived on the scene and threw a cordon around the area, the killer had escaped. A short start was all the cunning fellow needed.

Senior officers and medical staff were next to arrive. Lodging houses in the neighbourhood were searched and a telegram was sent to Scotland Yard to inform them of the crime. Although the murder had taken place in Whitechapel, it was considerably to the south of any of the other murders.

Doctors Allen and Phillips examined the now deceased body. Her throat had been severed to the spinal column. The wound ran from right to left and the gash was jagged. Great force must have been used.

The scene of the crime was searched and eighteen yards from the body was found 2 shillings wrapped in old newspaper. The corpse was bareheaded and the hair was disordered, indicating that a struggle had taken place. Superintendent Thomas Arnold of H division, concluded that 'there is nothing to connect this money with the murder nor has any instrument or article been found likely to afford a clue'.

The victim was a pathetic creature. Apparently, 'The whole of her clothing she was wearing at the time she was found was of the commonest and shabbiest description, while the heels had been almost entirely worn off her boots'. In her pockets were an old comb and some rags, but no money. A new hat was found in the folds of her dress and an old one was nearby. It was on 14 February that the victim was identified. She was Frances Coles, a twenty-six-year-old prostitute who had inhabited Whitechapel since 1883, living in common lodging houses. She had once worked in a pill factory but had found the work tedious. James Coles, her father, identified her corpse, as did her sister, Mary Ann. The latter said that her sister was poor and 'was of drunken habits', and earned about 7 shillings a week. She was later buried in Plaistow Cemetery, where four of the women killed in 1888 were also buried.

The police soon made an arrest, following information from one Samuel Harris. On the day after the murder, Inspector Henry Moore went to the Phoenix Pub, Upper East Smithfield, and found one James Thomas Sadler, a fifty-three-year-old ship's fireman. Sadler was a married man and said that he had known Frances for some time and had slept with her recently. He had been in her company on the evening before the murder but had argued with her before splitting

The Tower of London, c.1911, which overlooks the streets where Frances walked.
Reg Eden's collection

up. He then agreed to accompany the police officers and gave a statement at the police station.

Sadler had been discharged from SS *Fez* on Thursday 11 February. That evening he went to the Princess Alice pub on the Commercial Street, and met Frances. They spent the night together at a lodging house. On the following day he gave her money to buy a new hat (the one found on her body). That evening he was attacked in the street and robbed by a group of men. Sadler quarrelled with Frances as she had not helped him during the assault. Penniless, he claimed he left her and went to the Docks to try and gain admission to his ship. But as he was drunk he was turned away and then was set upon by another gang of men. He was knocked down and kicked.

Arriving at the same lodging house in Dorset Street (Annie Chapman had also lodged in the same street in 1888, as had Mary Jane Kelly – and the latter was killed in her lodgings there) that he had slept at on the previous night, he saw Frances; she had arrived at about 10.00. She had been drinking and had no money. The two of them had to leave. This part of the story and the fact that Sadler was injured were corroborated by Samuel Harris, who was present at the lodging house. He left first, at about 12.30 and Frances left a few minutes later, according to Harris. Sadler then said he went to the London Hospital to have his injuries treated, arriving at about 5.00. He did not see Frances again, he said. On his way to the hospital he met a constable; the time was about 2.30 or 3.00. The constable,

The London Docks, c.1930. Thomas Sadler disembarked from his shop here and was later attacked outside the dock gates. Reg Eden's collection

aware of the murder, ran his hands over his body and could not find a knife. At the hospital his head wounds were dressed and on the following day collected his wages and went on another drinking spree.

However, some of Sadler's story might have been incorrect. The attack at the Docks was said by other witnesses to have occurred after his leaving the lodging house, at about 1.15. A constable related talking to Sadler at about 2.00, at a location only a few minutes walk from the scene of the crime. He was next seen at the lodging house at about 3.00, and was directed to the hospital. An hour later he was seen at a coffee shop. But whether Sadler was lying or was genuinely confused – he had been drinking throughout the day – is open to question. The latter seems likely, though.

The inquest lasted for a number of days and began on 14 February. One startling piece of evidence was that later on Friday morning Sadler had sold a knife to Donald Campbell, a sailor. The knife had a slight stain and when it was washed the water had a reddish appearance. The constables gave their evidence and Sadler told his story, corroborated as noted, by others. The corpse was formally identified.

The medical evidence produced a number of facts. The victim had been thrown violently to the ground as suggested by a number of injuries to the back of the head. Her throat was cut whilst she lay on the ground. One doctor believed that the killer held her head back by the chin whilst cutting the throat with his right hand. Another doctor thought the killer struck from the front. It was uncertain whether

London Hospital, c.1905. Sadler had his injuries treated here. Author's collection

the knife had crossed the throat twice or thrice. When the throat was cut, the body was tilted so the killer could avoid being bloodstained. Unlike the killings of 1888 the victim had not been strangled and the knife used to kill was blunt, not sharp.

Ellen Callana was the key witness at the inquest. She had been walking along Commercial Street towards the Minories with Frances at about 1.30 on the morning of the murder. They were approached by a man dressed like a sailor, very short, with a dark moustache and wearing shiny boots and blue trousers. This was not the bearded Sadler. Ellen refused to accompany him and he punched her. Frances accepted the man's offer, despite Ellen's warning, 'Frances, don't go with that man; I don't like his look'. Her friend took no notice and Ellen commented, 'If you are going with that man, I will bid you good night'. She watched the couple turn into Whitechapel Street and then she returned to a lodging house in Brick Lane.

Possibly the last person to see the victim before her death (other than the murderer) was William Friday, a carman employed by a railway company. When he was passing along Royal Mint Street at about 1.40, he saw a man and a woman in a doorway and noted that the woman wore a black hat. They were about forty or fifty yards from Swallow Gardens. He saw them there again a few minutes later. When shown the victim's hat he identified it as hers. Unfortunately, he did not see the man well enough to give a description of him because he could not see his face clearly. He was wearing a dark brown overcoat with a velvet collar and a hard broad-brimmed hat.

Yet the couple seen by Friday may not have been Frances and her client/killer. Kate McCarthy stated that she had been with her fiancé, Thomas Fowles, at that spot and remembered Friday's passing by them on two occasions. He backed her up and said that they left the place at about 2.10. If this is correct, then the killing must have happened very shortly afterwards and the murderer and his victim had probably only just reached the archway.

On 27 February, the inquest was concluded. The verdict reached was that Frances had been 'wilfully murdered by some person or persons unknown'. They thought that the police had done well in detaining Sadler, but that he was not guilty. Sadler was finally released on 3 March, to the cheering of the crowd.

The police certainly still thought that Sadler was responsible, however. He was their only suspect – an unnamed man had been briefly taken in for questioning but had been quickly released. They investigated Sadler's past and kept a watch on him for some years. Although a good seaman, as proved by his papers, Sadler was clearly a repellent character. Sir Melville Macnaghten described him in 1894 as 'a man of ungovernable temper and entirely addicted to drink and the company of the lower prostitutes'. He had once possessed a knife and, in about 1880, his wife had surreptitiously removed it from him. They had lived in numerous addresses in the poorer districts of London in the 1880s and Sadler had taken a variety of jobs, separating from her in November 1888. Once he had wanted to show her one of the sites where a Ripper victim had been killed. He was also of a violent disposition. After the murder he was reconciled with his wife and set up a shop in south London. Their lodger claimed Sadler hit his wife and threatened to kill her. In May 1892 he said he would cut her throat. James Moffatt, the lodger, claimed Sadler was 'a most violent, subtle and treacherous man'.

However, he could not have been the Ripper. First, he was too old – aged fifty in 1888 when most witness descriptions of suspects claimed the men were aged in their twenties or thirties. One of these witnesses was shown Sadler and did not recognize him as the man he had seen in 1888. More importantly, Sadler had been working on a ship on 17 August 1888 and discharged on 2 October 1888, which meant that he had an alibi for most of the Ripper killings of that time.

It is possible that Sadler was guilty of the murder of Frances. Circumstantial evidence is strong. He had a knife; he had quarrelled with Frances a few hours earlier, claiming she had not done much to help him when he was attacked for the first time, and he was last seen in the vicinity of Swallow Gardens. He had motive, opportunity and means. Furthermore, he was of a violent disposition.

Yet it seems unlikely. He was drunk and had recently suffered two beatings. He wanted somewhere to stay for the night and to have his injuries seen to. Perhaps he is more in need of sympathy than suspicion. But Ellen's statement about Frances being last seen with another man is perhaps more significant. She was last seen at 1.30. Her corpse was discovered about forty-five minutes later. Was she killed by the man who Ellen saw her with? Possibly. It depends how long their encounter took. Could she have been killed by another man shortly afterwards? Certainly, whatever happened at the scene of the murder must have been brief as witnesses claimed no one was there just after 2.00. The murder remained unsolved.

Was Frances Coles the Ripper's last victim? Initial press speculation thought so, as *The Times* commented that the killing was

> *committed in the same district, and the many similar circumstances surrounding this latest mysterious crime seem to point to its being the work of the same person. The place, the time, the character of the victim, and other points of resemblance, recall in the most obvious way the series of crimes associated in the popular mind with the so-called 'Jack the Ripper'.*

The *Illustrated Police News* also heralded Frances as 'The latest victim of Jack the Ripper' and gave the killing much prominence on front covers of two issues in February 1891, alleging 'The Whitechapel monster still at large'. Yet we should recall that newspapers were likely to try and boost sales by encouraging this belief. In many ways the Ripper was a phenomenon of the press and indeed the pseudonym 'Jack the Ripper' was probably invented by a journalist. Yet the murders were real enough.

Wensley was uncertain, writing, 'Whether the murderer was Jack the Ripper or not, he escaped'. He thought the crime was 'strikingly similar in method' and that the body had been 'mutilated in much the same fashion as the victims of the Ripper'. In this, of course, he was wrong, as the body had not been mutilated.

The evidence is mixed. Whitechapel was a rough district and throat cutting was a common method of murder at this time. Frances could have been killed by the rough customer she was last seen with. As said, this unknown man is a strong candidate. Prostitute murders are not uncommon and are often difficult to solve, as we shall see with other cases in this book. Sir Melville Macnaghten wrote, in 1894, 'Now the Whitechapel murderer had 5 victims – & 5 victims only'. He went on to list the five victims of 1888. Abberline believed, too, that they ceased with the death of Mary Jane Kelly on November 1888. Dr Phillips, who examined the corpse, claimed that judging by 'the nature of the wound, the posture and appearance of the body &c. he does not connect this with the series of previous murders which were accompanied by mutilation'. Yet Elizabeth Stride's body had not been mutilated – the killer presumably heard a man approaching and so fled before he could commence such. A similar instance had happened here, with Thompson arriving on the scene just after the crime had been committed.

Thomas Divall, later a senior policeman, stated in his memoirs that Thompson 'is believed to be the only constable who ever saw Jack the Ripper', and then goes on to relate an erroneous account of how Thompson saw a man 'with a bag in his hand, a little distance ahead, under a lamp' and then stumbled on the corpse. He thought that Frances was the last of the Ripper's seven victims. Dew disagreed, later writing, 'There was great excitement. Ripper panic was revived. My view was that this was a false alarm. There was a tendency – and a natural enough tendency – for years for a violent murder which was not followed by a conviction to be laid at his door.' Is it a co-incidence that the police file on Frances Coles was and is in the same bundle as the other Ripper files? Yet so are the files on two other women who were killed at this time and are almost certainly not Ripper victims (Rose Mylett and an unknown woman).

The other question to ask is, if Frances was killed by the Ripper, why did the murders stop after her death? No one was ever charged with the murders, it must be recalled. Did the killer die? Was he arrested on another charge? Did he emigrate? Was he put into an asylum? Serial killers seldom stop voluntarily. One theory which would seem to carry some weight is that Thomas Cutbush was the Ripper. He was tried in April 1891 with wounding Florence Johnson and trying to attack Isabella Anderson in Kennington, using a knife. He was sent to an asylum. Cutbush was mentally deficient and he did know the East End quite well, having been employed there. He was also acquainted with prostitutes and had contracted syphilis. He had studied medical books and his movements in the autumn of 1888 were unclear. He was known to stroll the streets at night, returning covered in mud. He may have been suffering from paranoia.

But if Cutbush was the killer, why did Abberline claim, in a newspaper article in 1903 that:

Scotland Yard is really no wiser on the subject [the identity of the Ripper] than it was fifteen years ago ... the authorities would have been only too glad to make an end of such a mystery, if only for their own credit.

One possible reason for this is that Cutbush's uncle was Superintendent Charles Cutbush, who committed suicide in 1896. Even so, the evidence against him is still minimal.

We will probably never know whether Alice and Frances were the Ripper's last victims. Certainly no one afterwards was even regarded as a possible Ripper victim. The Ripper's reign was over, but the shadow of this long dead murderer remains with us and may only be exorcised if his identity is definitively proved. This seems very unlikely. If either or both of these women were killed by the Ripper, then some theories about the killer's identity will have to be rethought. But, of course, they may not have been. Although we appear to know more about this series of murders, the truth is still just as elusive.

CHAPTER 17

The Murder of Marius Martin 1894

He was a big man, and I thought he was going to get hold of me, so I fired at him with a revolver, and struck him on the forehead.

The Café Royale, situated at the south end of Regent Street, in London's West End, was in the 1890s the haunt of wits and artists such as Oscar Wilde and his chums. Yet life was not always so gay there. It was visited by a murderer.

Henry Hays, a stove cleaner, was at work in Regent Street in the early morning of 6 December 1894. He saw a light on inside the Café Royale at 3.40 am. Yet he could see nothing suspicious. He tried to obtain entry between 4.00 and 7.00 am but was unable to do so. Meanwhile, inside, a shocking discovery was made. At about 6.00 am, Alexander Delogneau, a cellarman employed at the Café Royale, heard a knocking at a door. When he went to answer it, he discovered the unconscious body of Marius Martin, a powerfully built thirty-nine year old who was employed as a night watchman to guard the premises. He was a Frenchman and had worked there for some years. He was lying in the passageway which led to the Glasshouse Street entrance. Martin had suffered two terrible wounds which had resulted in two pools of blood near his head. Sawdust was later thrown over the blood. Delogneau felt Martin's pulse, which was natural, but the breathing was hurried and his eyes were closed. He raised the alarm and the wounds were bound up. Paul Coutois, head cellarman, then took charge and summoned Dr Axham, who arrived at 7.00 am. Although at first he thought it was apoplexy and he sent Martin to Charing Cross Hospital. However, he never recovered consciousness and died later that day, at 3.45 pm.

It was thought that Martin had been attacked by a person or persons who had concealed themselves within the premises, perhaps in the lavatories, as there was no indication that there had been a break-in. A door leading to Air Street was found closed but unlocked

Regent Street, where the Café Royale is located, c.1900. Author's collection

and this may have been the mode of exit for the killer(s). It was also noted that Martin's keys had been taken from his trouser pockets, but replaced in his coat pockets. Martin lived on the premises and his wife and several other employees slept there. None reported that they had heard anything during the night. Although the window of the office was broken, this probably was not significant.

The motive was uncertain. Initially the police suspected that this was a burglary which had gone wrong. Martin's corpse had been found near the cash box and the safe (which held a considerable amount of money, over £400) in the large hall, but neither of these had been broken into. It was thought that he must have been surprised by the killer(s), for there was no sign of any struggle having taken place. He probably did not surprise them in the act of attempted theft, therefore, and this theory was discounted. It is more likely that Martin himself was the target of the killer(s), actuated by some private reason. Could a colleague have killed him? Yet none of the employees were missing. All were questioned and the premises searched, but to no avail.

The inquest began at St Martin's Vestry Hall, Charing Cross, on 10 December. Mathilde Martin, the widow, was the first witness. She worked at the place as a barmaid and was a few years younger than her husband. She had last seen her husband when he went on duty on the evening of 5 December. Martin was unarmed. Richard Crossman was the cashier at the Café Royale and he stated that he saw Martin at 1.05 am on the morning of the murder when he handed the door keys to Martin. He then had supper at about 2.30. Delogneau was the next witness and he recounted finding the body. He also said that he thought that a cab was waiting for some time outside the place, which was an unusual occurrence at that time of the morning, but whether this was connected with the murder, he could not say. In any case, would a killer put himself at the mercy of a cabman who might reveal his identity?

Cuthbert Lockyer of Charing Cross Hospital gave the medical evidence. The cause of death was two revolver bullets which entered the back of the head. Only one had been needed to kill him – the one which entered the right-hand side of his head. He thought that the bullets had been fired at almost point-blank range – about six inches from the head, in fact. He could not have killed himself (no weapon was found nearby). Martin had been shot at about 3.00 am. The inquest concluded on the following day with the verdict that Martin had been murdered by person or persons unknown.

The tragedy was made worse by the fact that, in August, Martin had acquired the freehold of a vineyard in his native Burgundy. Although he had wanted to leave his present job and return home, his wife had suggested that 'he see the year out' at the Café Royale. Martin agreed.

There was a sequel to the mystery, almost two decades later. Frederick Bedford, a fifty-three-year-old labourer of no fixed abode, confessed to the murder in Liverpool and detectives from London were dispatched to interview him. Bedford said that he had been born in Exeter and at the time was tramping around the country. He wrote a signed confession and part of it read as follows:

On the evening of the 4th I concealed myself under a seat, and about 2.00 am the following morning I came out of my hiding place when I saw the watchman. He was a big man, and I thought he was going to get hold of me, so I fired at him with a revolver, and struck him on the forehead. He never rose, and I heard a noise overhead, so I broke one of the panes of glass over the door leading to Glasshouse Street and got away.

Bedford claimed he had entered the Café Royale in order to steal any money he could find there. He found none, however. He then kept the revolver for some time until he gave it to a man of the name of Fowler who later killed the elderly Henry Smith at Muswell Hill. His motive for the confession was that he was getting older and wanted to make a clean breast of his crime before he died.

Once he was back in London, Bedford was charged. However, Detective Inspector Fowler examined the confession and did not think it rang true, claiming that it was 'found not to be in accord with the facts of the case'. This was presumably because Martin was killed by two bullets, not one as Bedford claimed. Bedford was then discharged.

It is impossible to know now who killed Martin. One modern theory is that one or more employees of the Café Royale killed him, arguing that Martin was an unpleasant character and had got some of his fellows into trouble and even had one sacked for a relatively minor offence. An apprentice cook recalled seeing a short, fat man waiting in a toilet on a previous night and saw the light burning in the same place on the night of the murder. This is certainly possible. At the very least, some collusion probably took place, as it seems very odd that no one heard anything on the night of the murder – two gun shots would have sounded even louder in the early hours if the morning. Nor had there been any sign of a forced entry. That the motive was a private matter and the killing was deliberate also seems likely, rather than it being a case of burglars, as nothing was taken and Martin was crept up upon before the revolver was fired at him. But all this speculation does not bring us closer to whoever pulled the trigger.

CHAPTER 18

Who Murdered Sarah Higgs? 1895

Only think that while we have been wondering where she was or where she could have got to, that she was lying here in the canal within sight of our windows, only fifty yards away and we knew nothing about it.

For the middle classes, the nineteenth century was a golden age for servants. Most professional people, as well as those of independent means, possessed at least one; most had two or three domestic servants. These were usually female, so could not command the wages of their male equivalents. Kensington apart, in the late Victorian era, Ealing had the most servants per head of population. In 1911, there were 68 servants per 100 households, compared to 23 per 100 in London. The lot of servants was variable, but few the fate of Sarah Jane Higgs.

In the local press, in late February 1895, came the following paragraph:

> *At the beginning of last week much painful excitement was caused in Yiewsley and the surrounding locality, by the discovery, in the Grand Junction Canal, near Horton Bridge, of the dead body of Sarah Jane Higgs ...*

Sarah had been born in about 1870 at Yiewsley, Middlesex, and her parents still resided there in 1895, at Thatcher's Cottages, near Horton Bridge. In fact, since the summer of 1894, she had been employed as a housemaid at Mrs Josephine Draper's house at Mount Park Road, Ealing, and received an annual salary of £16, paid monthly. She appeared to be 'a quiet, well behaved, respectable young woman' and her mother said she was cheerful and industrious (it was and is very rare for anyone to say anything against the character of a murder victim). As a child she had attended the Church National School, leaving aged thirteen. She had then worked as a servant in various posts – at the West Drayton stationmaster's, then at Uxbridge, then in London, before working in Ealing. Crucially, she had worked at a house in Hartington Road, Ealing, in 1891.

That her character was golden was not strictly true. She had given birth to an illegitimate son, one Henry John, on 4 October 1891, and the father (whose identity was not stated on the child's baptism record) acknowledged the baby as his, contributing towards its maintenance until the baby's death early in the following year. The father was unknown, but was said to be a man who lived near her mother's house, though this is not certain. Furthermore, she was three months pregnant at the time of death – or, as the newspapers delicately put it, 'her mistress had reason to suspect her condition'. In fact, Mrs Draper had intended to speak to her on this matter.

She never had the chance. On the evening of Thursday 2 January 1895, Sarah left the house. At first this went unnoticed. Thursday was her usual evening off and she had talked to Matilda Baker, a fellow servant, of catching the 8.17 pm train to visit her parents at Yiewsley and returning by 10.00 pm, which was when she was required to be at her employer's. There would have been time for her to have made a short visit and then to return. West Drayton Station was and is only about ten minutes walk at most from where her parents lived. She had been wearing a round sailor hat, a dark dress and jacket and a white silk handkerchief. She also stated that the reason for the visit was to visit a dressmaker there, which would have been either Miss or Mrs Belch.

What happened on the evening of 2 January is impossible to say with complete certainty. What is clear is that she did not travel by the 8.17 pm train, as she was seen in Ealing Broadway just before 9.00 pm. It would have then been impossible for her to have gone to Yiewsley and returned for 10.00 pm. Such behaviour was unusual and Sarah had never acted in this way before, except when she had to take a few days off in the previous August, due to illness. On the following day, Sarah's sister came to Mrs Draper's house and took away Sarah's belongings, though no money was found, despite Sarah being said to be reasonably affluent. Mrs Draper found some medicine bottles in her employee's room and a half-finished letter to her half-sister, concerning some trinkets she planned to give to her. None of those who knew her at Yiewsley had seen her there. Meanwhile, the police made enquiries at lodging houses without any positive result.

It was on 25 February that Thomas Clayton, butcher and fruiterer of Yiewsley High Street, made a shocking discovery. He had been walking along the canal tow path, near Horton Bridge, less than 100 yards from where Sarah's mother lived, and saw what he at first thought to be a bundle of rags floating in a gap in the ice-covered

Horton Bridge, 2005. Sarah's corpse was found near this site. Author's collection

water. He thought nothing of it and passed by. However, on passing the same way again, later in the day, he examined the object and found that it was a corpse. PC Cruikshank was summoned and took possession. Among the crowd who gathered there, a man shouted, 'There has been foul play here'. The corpse's outer skirt had been removed but otherwise it was fully clothed. The tragedy was noted by Martha Higgs, Sarah's mother, who said, 'Only think that while we have been wondering where she was or where she could have got to, that she was lying here in the canal within sight of our windows, only 50 yards away and we knew nothing about it.'

The inquest was held later that day at the De Burgh Hotel, very close to West Drayton Railway Station. After the body was identified and it was heard from Martha that the family had not seen her since August 1894, when Sarah had been ill, the main point under discussion was the cause of death. Dr William Hayden of Wycombe House, Yiewsley, said that the face and the lower part of the body were covered in mud from the bottom of the canal, but he thought that the corpse had not been held down in it. It was only slightly decomposed. He had also found, on closer examination, that there was a frontal head wound about one and a half inches long, which had broken one bone and fractured another. There was also a wound at the back of the head, which had not broken any bones. These blows had been inflicted when Sarah was alive, by a fall or a blow. She had not drowned, as there was no water in the lungs, but had been in the water for at least six weeks. The stomach was healthy, but there was no food in it. She was three months pregnant. The inquest was then adjourned in order to ascertain Sarah's last movements and to gather other pertinent information.

The adjourned inquest, which took place at the same location, but at which the police were present, was held a week later. Detective Inspector Nash and his colleagues had been making investigations into the matter in hand. The adjourned inquest lasted three hours. A number of witnesses were questioned.

The first was Mary Farr, a servant at Eccleston Road, Ealing Dean. She reported that she was a friend of Sarah's and that they often spent their leisure time together. On 16 December, on their way back from Acton, they met a man whom Sarah referred to as her 'young man', but she did not know his name. On the night of her disappearance, they had met in Ealing Broadway at 8.20 pm and walked to Ealing Common railway station, then back, meeting another female friend outside the Lyric Theatre on Ealing Broadway. Mary then left them at about 9.15 pm. She could not identify the man seen on 16 December, as she had only seen the back of his head. He was about thirty, had been wearing a light coat, black felt hat and

De Burgh Hotel, West Drayton, 2005. The inquest was held here. Author's collection

black trousers; possibly he worked in a shop. She added that Sarah seemed cheerful and did not think anything out of the usual was in the offing.

William Hammond, labourer of St Mary's Cottages, Yiewsley, stated that he had seen Sarah loitering near Horton Bridge early one morning, apparently looking for a lost possession – perhaps her outer skirt. He had known her for five years, but claimed he had never spoken to her, as 'I have got enough to do with the one at home'. When he returned to the same spot, twenty minutes later, she had vanished. Unfortunately he did not remember on what day it was, only 'after Christmas'.

Charles Butler of 3 Eastwood's Cottages, Yiewsley, who was possibly a labourer, had walked out with Sarah on three occasions in the summer of 1894. The last was on the August Bank Holiday. He had been with her and Ada, his sister, to the Lyric Theatre but, though 'we were friendly towards each other', he stressed that 'he was never guilty of any improper conduct' with her and that he 'did not know much' about her. He had not seen her since and did not know if she was seeing another man.

It certainly seems that Sarah was seeing another man and was on intimate terms with him. Ellen Downes, a servant working at Eaton Rise, and an old friend of Sarah's, said that Sarah intended to visit the Metropolitan Music Hall on Boxing Day 1894 and she was not going alone. She had expected to see Sarah on 30 December, but had not. Sarah's sister said that she knew who she was walking out with and referred to him as 'the biggest scamp out'. She did not identify him. This other man had been friends with Sarah since at least November, and this man was not Charlie – i.e. Charles Butler – as a servant recalled that Sarah said she had not seen him since August, which agrees with Charles's own account. There was uncertainty whether the man in question was from Ealing or not. Ellen certainly thought so, but others disagreed.

One possible clue – or red herring – came from Algernon Good-enough, booking clerk at West Drayton Station. He said that at 11.00 pm on 19 January he had heard a woman's screams from the direction of Horton Bridge. He thought it might be a domestic assault, though another witness said it was merely noise made by rowdy youths leaving a nearby pub, probably the Trout and Chequers. When Goodenough saw two constables, they said that the route was not on their beat, so could not investigate. Yet it was believed that Sarah had been starved for two weeks before entering the water, which would tally with Goodenough's statement.

Dr Hayden, who had had time to make another examination, was able to give further evidence. Another fracture at the front of the head was found. He said that the cause of death was shock to the nervous system caused by concussion to the brain and spinal cord, being caused by the blow to the back of the head. The body had been in the water for some time and so it was impossible to tell if all the blows had been made at the same time. There was some debate as to whether the death was suicide, caused by Sarah leaping from the bridge and hitting her head on the side of the bridge. Hayden said that Sarah was unconscious, but not dead when she entered the water. The jury only needed a short consultation before reaching the verdict of 'Wilful murder against some person or persons unknown'. Her mother was 'sure Sarah had been murdered and that she had been lured down there for that purpose'.

The killer was never found. The motive for the murder, though, is clear enough. Sarah was pregnant and she had told the prospective father about it. He was not in a position to marry her, or did not wish to do so. Perhaps he was already married or was in a situation in which the scandal of the result of his illicit affair would have been harmful. Could Sarah have been trying to blackmail him? He may have met her at the Lyric on 2 January, and suggested she go to West Drayton with him. Perhaps he suggested elopement or marriage? This would tie in with the absence of money in her room, as he may have suggested she take it with her. Having lured her there, he must have held her prisoner somewhere (but where? – perhaps a shed or outhouse – certainly nowhere that anyone might conceivably visit) for about two weeks, before deciding on what he should do. It is possible that 19 January was the date of the murder and, having wounded her, he threw her from the bridge, where she sank. The delay in the body being discovered was caused by the frosty weather, with ice covering the canal until late February.

Who killed her? Probably not Charles Butler, who had not seen her for months, though he did live near to the scene of the crime. William Hammond? Possibly, but probably not. He had motive (being married already) and was near the scene of the crime. He was vague about when he saw her, though this is not necessarily a sign of guilt and may be merely bad memory. He may have been her lover, but the question remains about where he hid her and how she could have been hidden for so long. As both men were labourers, they could hardly appear as the shopkeeper's assistant who had been identified as Sarah's beau. Unless, of course, they had changed into their Sunday best as one would when courting. It is a pity that Sarah's sister did not name her current lover.

Yet there was one more suspect, and a far more promising one. Although his identity was unknown, he was described thus:

*Height 5 ft. 8 in., black hair, dark moustache, with little side whiskers.
He wore a brown golf cap, and carried a slate covered waterproof coat
on his left arm, was attired in a brownish tweed frock coat, dark striped,
trousers and gaiters.*

His name was Harold and he was married, with five children, and
bore 'a good position'. He had been 'keeping company' with Sarah for
two years, having seduced her and spoke to her of marriage. Sarah's
baby was Henry, so it is not unlikely that the father could have been
named Harold. Apparently he was seen with her on the morning of
her disappearance at a pub in Little Ealing, presumably the Plough,
by a page boy who worked in Mount Park Road. He may have been
the same man that Mary Farr saw in the previous month. Yet is this
story true? Why was Sarah in Little Ealing, nearly two miles from
where she worked? It seems a long way (at least thirty minutes walk)
to go on an errand or with a message for her mistress.

Who was Harold? An examination of the young men named Harold
who were householders in Ealing in 1891 only comes up with two
names. One was Harold Lavey, but he was unmarried in 1891, and
the second was Harold Pryke and, although married, he had no
children. Both seem ruled out, therefore. There is another and more
probable man. This is Harry Dicconson, aged thirty-nine in 1891, a
commercial traveller, married and with seven children. Crucially, he
was Sarah's employer at Hartington Road in 1891. He certainly meets
all the criteria listed by the witness. Furthermore, as Sarah's employer, he would be able to exert a strong influence over her and
sexual relations between masters and servants were not unknown.
The Plough is about a mile from his home, so might have been a
convenient meeting place for them. The only argument against him
being her killer is that he seems a little old to be described as a young
man, when he would have been forty-two in 1895.

Whether the police pursued this line of enquiry, we do not know.
No more was learnt in public of any police investigation which surely
must have followed the announcement at the inquest. We will probably never know the truth, though Dicconson seems the most likely
suspect.

CHAPTER 19

The Railway Murder 1897

The murder of Miss Camp was wholly without motive, and was no doubt perpetrated by some homicidal maniac.

Trains travel could be dangerous, as two of the characters in this book learnt to their cost. This was because many trains did not have corridors which communicated to the rest of the train. Instead there were compartments accessible only by the doors which opened onto the platforms. A killer and his victim could therefore be alone without the latter having any chance of escape but with the former having every opportunity to leave without being discovered and detained. As Major Arthur Griffiths wrote in 1899:

Peculiar dangers have surrounded the newest method of locomotion . . . More particularly the insulation of a passenger in the old fashioned railway carriage, the difficulty of obtaining assistance, and the want of proper communication with others, have led to terrible crimes on the line.

On the evening of Thursday 1 February 1897, the 7.42 train from Hounslow was pulling into its final destination, Waterloo. It was 8.25 pm and it had previously stopped at Isleworth, Brentford, Kew Bridge, Chiswick, Barnes, Putney, Wandsworth, Clapham Junction and Vauxhall. Yet this was to be no ordinary arrival. In one of the second-class compartments was the dead body of a woman – the first woman to be murdered on an English train. Some newspapers called this 'the four minute murder' because it took four minutes to travel between Putney and Wandsworth, the stretch in which the murder was supposed to have been committed.

The victim was Miss Elizabeth Camp, who had been the house-keeper of the Good Intent Tavern, East Street, Walworth, for the last two years. She was well dressed, attractive and thirty-three years old. Previously she had been a barmaid at the same pub, from 1885 to

Waterloo Railway station, where the train with Elizabeth's Camp's body made its final call. John Coulter's collection

1889, then worked as a nurse at the Great Northern Hospital in Winchmore Hill until 1895. She had been engaged to Edward Berry, a Walworth fruiterer in 1896. They had known each other for sixteen years previously. It was he who had been waiting, by appointment, at Waterloo for her to return. This was to discuss the calling of the banns at St Paul's, Hammersmith's Parish Church, for they were to wed on 28 March that year. Her employer, Alfred Harris, the pub landlord, gave her a good reference and said she had only been out late at night twice: when she was visiting her sick mother and when she was on holiday in Hastings.

On the Thursday afternoon, just after seeing her fiancé, Elizabeth had boarded a train at Waterloo, at about 2.00 pm, in order to visit relatives. She was described as 'in a most cheerful mood when she left him'. First she saw Mrs Annie Skeats, her sister, and her brother-in-law, a manager of a Hammersmith firm of clothiers. Then she went to Hounslow to see Mrs Haynes, her other sister, who ran a sweetshop there. She took a train from Hammersmith at 4.15 pm and spent two hours with Mrs Haynes, from about 5.00 pm, and it was she who then saw Elizabeth off at the railway station. The latter entered a second-class compartment of the train, where she was the sole occupant. Elizabeth insisted on travelling second class because there one met a better class of passenger, though her sister warned 'That may be so, but the third is safer for women'. Mrs Haynes thought that her sister

Hammersmith Church, c.1900, where Elizabeth was to have married in the following month. Author's collection

seemed in good spirits. The head porter recalled that few passengers were travelling on that train and he remembered Elizabeth's entry into a second-class carriage. Elizabeth was last seen alive when the train stopped at Putney. She was reading a magazine and there was a man sitting opposite to her, though he was not described.

The body was discovered by a carriage cleaner after the passengers had all alighted at Waterloo. The corpse had been stuffed under a seat in that carriage. It was still warm and the 'head was shockingly battered'. There was no weapon at the scene of the crime. The corpse was taken by ambulance to Lambeth Parish Mortuary, where it was identified an hour later by Berry.

Both the CID and the police employed by the London and South Western Railway Company began to investigate the murder on Thursday night. But the investigation was hindered by the fact that the railway carriage in which the murder had been committed had been cleaned up as soon as the body had been removed, so there was no possibility of finding any clues there. The police began by searching the railway line from Hounslow to London. When they reached Mount Pleasant, between Putney and Wandsworth, on the following day, they found on the embankment on the side of the line a chemist's pestle with blood and hair on it.

This was clearly the murder weapon, as Elizabeth's head had been brutally battered by a bludgeon of some kind. It seemed likely that she was killed between Putney and Wandsworth and the weapon was then thrown from the carriage window. The pestle was heavy and had not been bought recently. It had a figure 6 or 9 on it, depending on which way up it was. The pestle was perhaps the one which was sold as part of the effects of a recently deceased Brompton doctor. A dealer recalled that the buyer 'carefully balanced it in his hand and, made a remark about its weight'. However, another account claimed that it was of the type which was used for gold-beating and the dealer, one Mr Cavanagh of Somers Town, said he had sold one to an American who had been lodging at his house for several months and who knew Elizabeth. This dealer also claimed that Elizabeth and the purchaser were married, but there is no evidence for this. Yet he claimed to recognize her corpse when he was shown it. After his brief spell in the limelight, Cavanagh disappeared. Presumably he was not involved in the murder. A final version of the story states that a Mr Haisman of Cowcross Street said that one of his pestles was stolen from his shop in August 1896. He said that such were used for brass and gold work on yachts at Southampton.

Another odd clue was found, this time in the restaurant at Waterloo Station. The speaking tube between the restaurant and the kitchen was blocked. Upon investigation, a handkerchief was located there, bearing the name 'E. Camp' and, coincidentally, Elizabeth's handkerchief was missing. However, there had been an employee of the restaurant with that name, so this does not necessarily imply that someone connected with the restaurant was guilty. Furthermore, the handkerchief was not identified by any of Elizabeth's friends.

It was unknown, though, why she had been killed. Berry did not know the answer, but wondered if it might have been financial, as she often carried large sums of money on her person, but he was not really sure because he was unaware of how much she had been carrying. Yet Mrs Haynes thought this was definitely not the case, because they had gone shopping in Hounslow and her unmarried sister remarked that she had spent nearly all her money (presumably the goods had been ordered to be sent to her, rather than being carried away directly). Furthermore, Elizabeth's brooch, earrings and silver mounted umbrella had not been taken. The only items missing were the aforesaid handkerchief, a green purse, a small sum of money and the railway ticket from Hounslow.

Superintendent Robinson of the railway company's police reconstructed the crime thus. He stated that Elizabeth entered a second-class carriage at Hounslow and sat with her back to the engine. But, it was not known at which station her assailant boarded the train. After he did, he probably struck her a blow on the forehead to try and stun her. She probably resisted, for she was a strong girl and well built, weighing thirteen stone. Her umbrella had been broken and there were splashes of blood on the other side of the compartment – presumably her killer's.

The killer then struck her a second blow on the left side of her face, smashing her skull and killing her. She was pushed under the seat, lying on her back with her legs across the floor of the carriage. The killer probably got out at Wandsworth station.

Suspects were numerous. Inspector Marshall thought that a 'gang of loafers who infest the western end of the Hanworth Road' might be responsible. Then there were a number of rumours circulating about mysterious men seen leaving the railway stations en route. Some had cut hands. Another man was allegedly seen at the Alma pub at Vauxhall. He came in at 8.30 pm for brandy. A barmaid later said:

> He appeared to be in a nervous and excited state . . . he trembled as he lifted the glass containing the brandy to his mouth, and some of the liquor was spilt. I would say he was about thirty-five years of age, or perhaps a little more. He wore a long dark macintosh and bowler hat, and one of his fingers was tied with a piece of rag. He was accompanied by a cab [driver], and after a few minutes, they left.

They then travelled into London. The man was later identified as Austin Woods of Stockwell, a manager of a bicycle shop. The injury had been caused when he was repairing a client's bicycle. He was cleared from enquiries.

Another story concerned a man with blood on his clothes. A man left the train at Wandsworth with a bloodstained waistcoat, though he said it was spilt furniture polish and he offered onlookers drinks. They refused. He was never seen again. At Clapham Junction, a man was seen leaving the station with his hand bound up.

On investigation, none of the stories yielded anything fruitful. A few days later, a man confessed to the crime, but the police were doubtful of his truthfulness and sanity and did not attach much importance to his statement. Another possibility was an unnamed thief who often jumped on and off trains and made thefts from passengers. He had recently changed his lodgings and was difficult to track down. One Marshall, a young man from Reading who was a publican's son, was taken in for questioning. He had been in Guildford for a few days, to buy a false moustache prior to enlisting in the army. He was released after questioning.

A more probable suspect was Thomas Stone, a Hounslow resident. He was a friend of Mrs Haynes and had spent some time on the evening of the murder with Mrs Haynes and Elizabeth. The three of them had been at a hotel before the two women left to go to the railway station. Stone's movements from that time until midnight were unknown. He was brought in for questioning, but could not be held indefinitely because there was no evidence against him, so was released. A barber by the name of Doman, who lived near Mrs Haynes, was seen as a rival of Stone's for Elizabeth. He was not seen as a potential killer, but the police questioned him.

Edward Berry could not have been guilty as Thomas Berry, his brother, and George Forest, a fellow grocer, provided him with an alibi, as they had been with him at 7.00. A previous lover of Elizabeth, one William Brown, a barman at the Prince Albert on Walworth Road, was also cleared. They had seen each other for a few months in 1895, but parted amicably. Apparently he had failed to turn up to a couple of meetings with her and the whole affair fizzled out. On the evening of the murder, he had been in the pub, serving customers.

Fred Burgess, a pastry chef, had been on the train on the night of the murder. He saw a man leaving a second-class compartment at Wandsworth, where, he, too, had alighted. He described him thus:

He was a man of medium height, about 5 foot 6 or 5 foot 7. He wore a top hat and a frock coat. He had a dark moustache. The only unusual thing about him was his hurry. I noticed his face as we went down the stairs on the first landing, and should know him if I saw him again. I should think he was from twenty-seven to thirty – under thirty. His coat was black, and it may have been a short overcoat.

At the inquest, a juror suggested that the railway company offer a reward for the arrest of the murderer. The foreman of the jury recalled that such a reward had led to the arrest of a killer in America. The coroner, though, was doubtful, arguing that rewards often led to the supplying of false information in order to obtain the reward money. Meanwhile the jury viewed the body and looked at the railway compartment where Elizabeth had been killed. The inquest was adjourned, but on its conclusion in April nothing substantial was learnt as to who killed Elizabeth or why. The railway company offered a reward of £200 for anyone who could give information leading to an arrest, but no one was able to claim it.

The postscript to this story occurred in 1906, when one Robert Clive, a private soldier serving in South Africa, confessed to the crime when he was in a military prison for burglary. He was transported back to London to be interviewed by the senior police officers who had taken charge of the Elizabeth Camp case in 1897. However, they concluded that his confession was 'a tissue of falsehoods written to deceive the military authorities and with the prisoner's being sent to England'. He was escorted back to South Africa. According to his mother, he was 'a good for nothing, wicked son'.

One later theory was that a medical student, motivated by sexual desire, killed her. He might have had access to a pestle. A similar theory is that a man had been attracted to Elizabeth whilst she worked at the hospital, but she did not reciprocate his advances. He began to pester her with his attentions, so much so that she left the hospital to work in the pub. The man was never found. Yet to wait two years before committing this murder out of revenge seems unlikely. Furthermore, how could he have known she would have been on that train at that time?

Another theory was that a lunatic was responsible. One writer thought that the killer might have been a dangerous criminal who had just been released from prison. He was later convicted of a murder in which he had used a leaden window weight as a weapon. Unfortunately this theorist does not name her killer. Sir Melville Macnaghten interviewed a man found wandering on Blackheath. He was mentally defective, travel stained, unshaven, sleeping rough and lacking an overcoat. There was no proof he was anywhere near the scene of the crime and was not identified by any of the possible witnesses. The man was not charged, but was put into an asylum.

Elizabeth Camp's murder is inexplicable. No one is known to have had a grudge against her. Yet if her murder was a spur of the moment crime, why did her killer come with a pestle, which is not a usual implement to carry around? There seems to be no rational motive. Could the killer have been suffering from paranoia or schizophrenia?

This would certainly explain an otherwise motiveless murder of a stranger. As Macnaghten wrote:

The murder of Miss Camp was wholly without motive, and was no doubt perpetrated by some homicidal maniac. Such men, I believe, have no recollection of their guilty acts, which pass out of their minds as soon as they have been committed.

CHAPTER 20

Open Window, Open Door to Crime
1898

Notwithstanding the verdict, and the fact that two months have elapsed since the date upon which the poor lady was murdered, the police have by no means lost all hope of securing the assassin.

According to the *Kentish Mercury* of 19 August 1898: 'In the early hours of Monday morning a terrible tragedy, the more shocking by reason of the fact that it is at present, and indeed, is likely to be, perhaps for ever, shrouded in the deepest mystery, occurred at Kidbrook.'

Mrs Arabella Charlotte Tyler was a wealthy middle-aged widow who lived in a detached house on Kidbrooke Park Road, near Blackheath. The house stood in its own grounds and was approached by a winding carriage drive. Behind it lay open agricultural land, lonely lanes and footpaths. Mrs Tyler was a devout and regular churchgoer at the nearby St James's and was known for her charitable gifts to the local poor. She was widely respected in the locality. Her husband had been William John Tyler, once secretary of the India Rubber and Gutta Percha Telegraph Company, of Silvertown. Since his death she had lived with her grown-up daughters and Mary Ann Gustusson, the cook.

On the evening of Sunday 14 August 1898, Mrs Tyler went to bed at her usual hour. None of her three daughters (Maud Lilian Tyler, Violet Louise Huxham and Margaret Mary Stuart Childs) were with her. Her bedroom was immediately above the dining room and the open window was directly above the front door. Over the door was a porch and above that was an iron trelliswork, covered with a Virginia creeper. Mary locked all the ground-floor doors and windows before retiring to bed herself at about 10.45 pm; half an hour after her

BLACKHEATH, KIDBROOK CHURCH AND SHOOTERS HILL IN DISTANCE.

Kidbrooke Church, c.1920s, where Arabella Tyler was a regular worshipper, is in the background. Author's collection

mistress had done so. Locking up was normally a job for the housemaid, but the household was lacking one at the time. She slept in a room on second floor and was a light sleeper.

Next day she rose at about 6.30 am and began her daily duties. However, when she went downstairs she was surprised to find that internal doors were ajar and that the kitchen door leading to the garden was wide open. The gas fire had been lit and the plate cupboard was open. Neither had been so, late the previous night. Perhaps this had been the work of her mistress who had said she might rise at 5.00 am on that morning. Even so, not seeing her in the garden, she was puzzled, so then went upstairs to report this to her mistress and to fetch her a glass of hot water. The bedroom door was partly open, but Mary knocked all the same. Receiving no reply, she entered the room and was shocked at the sight.

Her mistress, clad in her night-dress, was lying at the foot of the bed. Her arms were outstretched and her fingers were bent and rigid. Her head was thrown back and her face was discoloured. The body was cold. Losing no time, the shocked woman ran to Miss Bayley, a friend of her mistress, and she contacted the local police and sent for a doctor.

Dr Clifford accompanied the officers. He examined the body and pronounced that life had been extinct for a number of hours. Death was due to manual strangulation. Whoever had committed the crime must have had very powerful fingers, judging by the indentations on the neck.

The police then made a thorough search of the house and the land adjacent to it. In the kitchen, a number of drawers had been opened. However, though they searched all the rooms in the house, they could not find any trace of anything having been stolen. Leaving the house, they proceed to inspect the grounds. The large French windows which opened into the dining room had been tampered with, presumably in an unsuccessful attempt to break in that way. However, an examination of the trelliswork showed how the criminal had entered the house, through the open window. The creeper there had been torn and there were dirty finger marks on the bedroom's verandah. So much for his entrance.

It was clear that the man had left by the back kitchen door. Footprints were found in the flower beds and these led as far as the fence bordering the property. However, the tracks could not be followed further than that because, due to the recent hot weather, the ground was too hard for any traces to be found. Scotland Yard detectives took plaster casts of the footprints which were found, however.

The inquest began on 17 August at Kidbrooke Mission Room, not far from the scene of the crime. Many more relevant facts were brought to light. One was that, only a day before the murder, Mrs Tyler confided to friends that she was worried about burglars, though whether this was anything more than general fear was unknown. There had been some thefts of fruit from the garden, and a few hens had been taken in the past.

The first witness was Samuel Childs who lived in Hendon, and was one of her sons-in-law. He thought that the jewellery in his mother-in-law's house was of little value, though the plate was valued at £220. He was aware of the petty thefts mentioned above, but had not seen Mrs Tyler since June and could add little else.

Mary spoke next. Understandably, she was in a distressed state and had to sit down whilst giving evidence. She told the court of a visitor to her late mistress, who had arrived on the Sunday evening. This was one Mrs Georgina Jackson, a fifty-two-year-old widow who lived on Shooter's Hill, who paid two visits; one at 6.15 and the other at 7.45 pm. Each time she stayed for about ten minutes. Mary had never seen this woman before. Oddly enough, Mrs Jackson does not seem to have been called as a witness.

She then described her discovery of the body. She did not think her late mistress was a light sleeper and said that the bedroom window was often open, as it had been on the night of the murder. This was presumably because of the heat. It had been open about a foot, she thought. The bed had not been interfered with, with the bed-clothes having been simply thrown back.

Dr Cooper, the divisional surgeon, was the next witness. Death had occurred between 2.00 and 3.00 am on Monday morning. Some blood would have issued from the nose and mouth as the woman died, and he noted that the killer had wiped his hands in a bowl of water which was in the room. The doctor thought that death had been quick and occurred on the bedroom floor, rather than on the bed as the latter was undisturbed. Contents of some of the drawers in the room had been disturbed and the room was in some disorder, but it seemed as if nothing was missing, except, possibly, for a few shillings. Two valuable rings, for instance, had been in view, but had not been removed.

The police concluded that 'The evidence we have to work upon at present is very slight indeed. In fact the police have nothing to work upon.' The inquest was therefore adjourned. The police questioned several men about the crime, but all were released shortly afterwards.

Additional clues were few. A poker, taken from the kitchen, was found in the shrubbery. Near to this was a bunch of keys, which had not belonged to Mrs Tyler. Neither of these finds proved to be helpful.

Theories abounded. One of the wilder ones was that this was a repeat of the story written by Edgar Allan Poe, *The Murders in the Rue Morgue*, where two women are strangled in their home. The killer transpires to be an escaped baboon. Another possibility was that a woman was responsible. Yet another was that the burning of a hay-stack in a nearby farm was the work of accomplices of the criminal, to act as a method of distracting anyone from the crime. This seemed unlikely, but it might have led to the criminal hiding in the bushes before venturing out again, which is perhaps why the keys and poker were found there.

The inquest was concluded in October. Despite the efforts of Chief Inspector Conquest, insufficient evidence had been found to make a case against anyone. There was no new evidence to put before the jury. Therefore the coroner decided to allow the jurors to ask pertinent questions. Mr Fitt asked Mary whether she had ever had any male visitors to see her. Although this was thought to have been an irregular question, the witness said that she had not; the only visitor she had had whilst she had worked there was a female cousin, and that some three months prior to the murder. Fitt was adamant that this was a relevant question and that rumours gained from questioning had, in the past, furnished the police with key clues.

There was also discussion about the fact that the door to the plate cupboard in the kitchen was open, when it had been locked on the previous day. Mary said that she had a key to that cupboard, but that there might have been others. It was then stated that Mrs Tyler had had a key which opened this cupboard.

The verdict was 'wilful murder by person or persons unknown'.

The basic outline of events is clear enough. A man, probably a 'professional' and experienced burglar, knew of Mrs Tyler's wealth and was watching the house, waiting for its occupants to be at their lowest number. He struck when the daughters were absent. His first plan was to enter via the French windows on the ground floor, perhaps by using some form of lockpicking device. When this failed, he climbed into Mrs Tyler's bedroom, using the trellis. It was unfortunate that the trellis provided this means of entry and that that route led him into Mrs Tyler's room. He may not have anticipated this. Mrs Tyler awoke and the criminal then killed her – though it is unlikely that murder was his original intent. He then left the house in a noiseless manner (Mary was a light sleeper and swore she heard nothing), and without taking anything, though he did look through a few drawers in the kitchen before doing so, perhaps to find a key for the back door. He then left, having failed in his felonious intent and having committed a capital offence. He was probably an agile and strong man, having climbed up the trellis and having killed using such force.

Or could the motive have been financial? Mrs Tyler was a wealthy woman – on death, her net estate was worth £5,869. She had made a new will on 29 September 1897. However, the contents of the will do not provide an obvious motive for murder. Apart from a couple of small legacies to her relations, the bulk of the estate went to her three daughters, but most of this was put into a trust from which the three women could only enjoy the interest from the investments made from the capital sum. This would provide an income for them, but no one stood to gain a significant amount immediately. Nor did Mary or Mrs Jackson gain anything. Therefore, this does not seem to provide an adequate motive for murder on their behalf.

As for the police, it was a great pity that fingerprinting was at a primitive level and hardly ever used at this time. Even so, fingerprints are only of use if the suspect is caught and his fingerprints taken and compared with those found at the scene of the crime. Had the criminal been an offender previously known to the police and had a set of his prints been taken, an arrest would have been possible. But as it was, there were no witnesses and the man did not give himself up. In this scenario, unless there was a confession, the police's task was next to impossible. The final comment in the local newspaper seems rather optimistic:

Notwithstanding the verdict, and the fact that two months have elapsed since the date upon which the poor lady was murdered, the police have by no means lost all hope of securing the assassin, and the opinion is expressed in high police quarters that an arrest in the near future is by no means an impossibility.

None was forthcoming, however, and the mystery was recalled in 1931 at the time of another mysterious murder on Blackheath (detailed in the author's *Foul Deeds and Suspicious Deaths in Deptford and Lewisham*).

Chapter 21

The Death of a Polish Prostitute (1) 1903

Dora said that she was frightened to sleep alone.

At the beginning of the twentieth century, there were about 30,000 Poles and Russians in Britain and most of them lived in London. One was Mrs Dora Piernick, nee Zigelman, who had married a shoemaker in 1893. Ten years later, this twenty-eight-year-old Jewess from Lodz, in Polish Russia, may have thought she was a cut above many prostitutes, who lived, at best, in common lodging houses where the nightly rent was 4 pence. Again, unlike many, she was well dressed, blonde and attractive. Her current occupation was due to economic necessity. The couple had come to England and fell on hard times. Her husband turned to crime and was arrested and gaoled. She had her own room, on the ground floor of a house in Whitfield Street, 'a long dingy, alien haunted thoroughfare off the blazing Tottenham Court Road'. In 1903, while her husband was in prison, she was to share the fate of other prostitutes whose deaths are chronicled in this book. Ironically, on 22 June 1891, and probably unbeknown to Dora, one Elizabeth Stoffel, a prostitute, had been killed in the same street by one Paul Acheton.

It was Tuesday 29 December 1903. One of the last people to see Dora alive was Abraham Cohen, a grocer. Dora had asked him if he could give her change for £8 in gold. He had told her that he had insufficient money for such a transaction. Dora then went to a restaurant in Upper Rathbone Place and put a similar question to Jane Barber, meeting a similar response.

The next to see her was Sarah Piernick, Dora's sister-in-law of Upper Rathbone Place, and of the same occupation. She saw her in Tottenham Court Road just before midnight. The two women talked for ten minutes. Here she showed her sister-in-law what money she had and talked of seeing her gaoled husband on the following day, intending to let him know that she had enough money to survive.

Whitfield Street, 2006, scene of the murder of Dora Piernick. Author's collection

Showing that she had money in such a public place may have been unwise. In any case, Dora was accompanied by a young man. He was clean-shaven and thin-faced, wore a light grey suit and cap, and was probably English. Dora told Sarah that she was about to go home. One Dora Goodman said she saw Dora Piernick alone at about midnight.

Annie Scowie of Tottenham Street, another Polish prostitute and an old friend of Dora's, was the next to see her; at about 12.30 am. Dora told Annie that she had a nice fire at home and that Sarah was welcome to share it with her and to spend the night there. Sarah declined and Dora then said that she would have something to eat at a restaurant first. There was no mention made of the young man seen with Dora by Sarah, so presumably their business had been transacted and he had disappeared, having paid his money.

No one is known to have seen Dora alive again. She presumably found another client and went back to her lodgings. Meanwhile, at the lodging house, Julian Bartelle, a Frenchman, and a bricklayer and stonemason by trade, who lived in the basement flat below Dora's, went to bed at 12.30 am. Half an hour later, he could hear Dora's door opening and someone entering. He fell asleep, despite sharing the room with two others.

His sleep was not to be uninterrupted however. At 6.00 am he heard a woman scream, followed by three loud shouts of pain. Then there was a loud thudding sound and the breaking of glass. Rising from bed, he opened his door, but could hear nothing else. He tried to rouse one of his room-mates, but to no avail and so decided to investigate himself. He went upstairs and listened at Dora's door. He heard some heavy breathing, but nothing more, so returned to bed and slept. Previously he had checked Dora's window, but no one was then using it as an exit from the house. Oddly enough, Henry Talbot, a hairdresser, and one of his room-mates, later claimed that he had heard two people enter the room above and then some inaudible conversation take place between them.

Rosa Pourvoyer was the wife of the house's landlord, Emile. She also heard noises in the night, which sounded like someone getting out of bed and going towards the window, upsetting something on the way. She thought it was merely lodgers arguing and said this to her husband. On the Wednesday afternoon, between 2.00 and 3.00 pm, a young man called for Dora. Rosa looked for Dora's key, which was usually to be found in the hallstand. It was missing. She went up to Dora's room, but finding no response, assumed that she must be out and told her visitor so.

It was only later that day that concern grew about Dora. Police Sergeant Thomas Clark came to the property and broke the door down. The room was in darkness. One window was open and the other had its shutter closed. On looking at the bed, he saw Dora's body, lying there with its knees drawn up and the head and shoulders bare. Her throat had been cut and there were two pools of blood on the floor. After calling for a doctor, he made an examination of the room. It was neat and orderly, though the glass chimney of a lamp near to the open window had been broken. There was no sign of any struggle. Could this have been a case of suicide? Yet, there were two things he could not find – the key to the door and the weapon used to commit the crime.

Two men examined the corpse. The first of these was Dr Samuel Lloyd. There were wounds on the front and the left side of the throat. A towel had been placed beneath the left shoulder and this had caught some of the blood. Lloyd thought that death would have been slow – anything from a half an hour to two hours after the wound had been inflicted. He thought that the body had been lifted onto the bed after the fatal wound had been struck. He also noticed that there was bruising on the knees and other parts of the body, probably caused by a fall. Lloyd concluded that suicide should not be ruled out because there was no sign of a struggle occurring in the room and because of the nature of the wound – inflicted from left to right, which is how a right-handed person would naturally commit suicide.

A few days later, a Home Office pathologist, Mr Augustus Pepper of Wimpole Street, made a post-mortem examination. He noted that the wound was not a deep one, and though the jugular vein had been cut, the facial and lingual vessels were intact. Death had been caused by the slow loss of blood from the neck. He, too, thought that the nature of the wound pointed to suicide.

The inquest was held on 4 January at St Pancras' Coroner's Court before Walter Schroeder, deputy coroner for central London. The witnesses were called and gave their evidence. Sarah said that Dora was relatively well off, having £8 in gold and a number of valuable rings. The latter were displayed in court and Sarah recognized them. Annie noted that Dora was wearing these rings when she last saw her, and also said that Dora was wearing a different hat to the one that Sarah had seen her wearing, only about forty minutes previously. Pourvoyer stated that he had borrowed some money from Dora on the day before she died. Dora was, therefore, fairly well off. Robbery, though, was probably not the motive. A police search of the room revealed that there were five rings and almost £8 in gold wrapped up in the bedding.

On a different footing, Dr Hill added that the noises heard by Bartelle might have been those of a dying person suffocating. The coroner then said that further time was needed in order for the police to examine the case. Although Lloyd and Pepper suggested that the death was a suicide, he pointed out the fact that the door was locked and yet no key could be found, and this, as well as the absence of any weapon, pointed to the likelihood of it being murder. He also wanted time for a proper autopsy and an analysis of the contents of the corpse's stomach to take place.

The inquest was concluded on 1 February. New witnesses were brought forward. The first was Pourvoyer, who gave an account of his movements. He said that, after the young man had called for Dora, he took his young daughter for a walk in Regent's Park. They went as far

Regent's Park, c.1910. Dora's landlord visited here after her murder. Author's collection

as the canal, but he did not dispose of anything there. Mr Jones, Pourvoyer's solicitor, stated that the police had followed his client's trail and had found nothing suspicious. He also said that it was incorrect, as Sarah had alleged, that Dora paid 22 shillings and 6 pence for her weekly rent. The true figure, he said, was 5 or 7 shillings.

Annie Cohen of Upper Rathbone Place, another prostitute, said that she had known Dora for five weeks, and had slept in her room on the Monday night. Intriguingly, she told how Dora said that she was frightened to sleep alone, but did not say why. This seems to agree with the evidence of the other prostitute, who said Dora had asked her to stay with her on the following night. She also noticed Dora's wealth. Was Dora frightened of someone?

Percy Hollister appeared to have vital evidence. He was employed by St Pancras council to clear the drains. On 12 January, he was employed on Whitfield Street and, 30 yards from the house where Dora had died, found a broken razor with a notched edge. Three days later he found three keys, a little further away from Whitfield Street. He handed all these in to the police. Unfortunately, these clues were worthless. Pepper said that the razor which Hollister had found would have produced a jagged wound, whereas the fatal cut was straight. The police had tested the keys on Dora's lock, but none fitted.

There was the question about whether poison of any type had been used. Dr Stevenson, a Home Office analyst, said that he could find no trace of poison. However, the use of chloroform to make Dora unconscious could not be ruled out, as it left no trace after a short while.

Perhaps the most curious witness was the thirty-one-year-old John Ross, a clerk living in Whitechapel. He had confessed to the murder. However, he was drunk at the time. On the following day he retracted the confession, claiming that he had never been to that address and had only read about the death in the press. After checking his story, and finding the confession to be a mere invention, he was dismissed.

There was further discussion as to whether it might be a case of suicide. Dora's friends said that she was cheerful, did not drink and never mentioned suicide. The police agreed. Inspector John Kane said there was no evidence that she was suicidal, though she was disappointed that she had been refused a permit to visit her husband in prison.

The jury then had to decide on the verdict. How did Dora meet her death? The coroner continued to state that the medical witnesses suggested that it might have been suicide, but, of course, it might have been murder. He suggested to them that they could return an open verdict if they were uncertain whether it was suicide or murder. This was indeed what the jury concluded, believing that the evidence was insufficient to reach either verdict. This open verdict meant that the police did not have to include this in their list of unsolved murders for 1903, making the total for that year nil.

One theory, as recounted by Sir Melville Macnaghten, was that Dora had committed suicide and this had been discovered by the landlord. Fearing that he might be accused of the murder, he took away the murder weapon and locked the door behind him, later throwing both away. Macnaghten thought this was improbable, writing, 'Possible, but not probable, I think'.

Yet it seems fairly clear that Dora was murdered. One witness heard two people entering the room; clearly one was Dora and the other her client/killer. Since no weapon or the door keys were found, suicide must be ruled out. Finally, two witnesses inferred that Dora was eager to have company and one said that she was worried about sleeping alone. Worried about whom? Clearly not the man she brought back to the room. Why was she killed? Not for financial gain, certainly. We do not know if sex took place. Was the killer a homicidal maniac or was there some other rationale behind the killing? Did the killer wish to have his revenge for Dora's criminal husband? Certainly the death was brutal – and slow. Why did Dora not cry out? Was she unconscious at the time of the assault and her death? Presumably she was.

CHAPTER 22

Did Robert Wood Kill Phyllis Dimmock?

1907

Although we must abide by the jury's decision, there is no moral doubt that Wood was guilty of the murder.

On the late morning of Thursday 12 September 1907, Bertram Shaw, a cook employed on the Midland Railway, had just finished his shift. He had been at work since 4.30 in the afternoon of the previous day and had been on the 7.20 am from Sheffield that morning. He went to his lodgings in St Paul's Road (now Agar Grove), Camden Town, letting himself in with his latch key. As planned, his mother was there. Both were surprised that the door to the bedroom was locked. Shaw broke it down. Once inside, he was in for another surprise. The chest of drawers had been ransacked, as if someone had been there, searching for something. On top of the chest of drawers was his razor. He then pulled back the bedclothes and saw a horrific sight.

There he saw the corpse of Emily Elizabeth Dimmock, with whom he had been living since January 1906. Emily was aged twenty-three and was known as Phyllis. She had been born into a large working-class family in Walworth. Initially she was employed in a straw hat factory at Wellingborough, but then she worked as a housemaid in East Finchley. It is thought that the drudgery bored her and she wanted an escape into a more glamorous life. This led to her walking the streets and she was euphemistically 'known to policemen in the locality, and was frequently seen in the company of men other than Shaw'. This was how she met Shaw and the two set up house together. Yet she was still a prostitute, and saw clients when Shaw was at work (he worked the night shifts on the railway, leaving for work in the evening and returning late mornings). He claimed to be unaware of this fact. A few items of jewellery were missing. He went to find a constable and a doctor.

Detective Inspector Neil went to the scene of the crime on the afternoon of its discovery. He saw Phyllis's naked body, lying on the bed.

The throat had been cut by a single blow by a sharp knife or razor, severing most of the muscles in the neck and nearly splitting the spinal cord. There were bloodstains on the sheets in the shape of finger-marks, which were photographed. There was no possibility of suicide. The murder had probably been done whilst the woman was asleep as no resistance seems to have been offered – no other marks on the body could be seen. The time of death was in the early hours of the morning. No one in the building had heard anything suspicious. Over the next few days, more clues came to light – one was a piece of paper with writing on it and the other was a postcard. Copies of these were published in the press in the hope that someone would recognise the handwriting and come forward.

Neil made enquiries and the clues seemed to point in one direction. On 4 October, he went in search of the suspect and found him, with a young woman, in Gray's Inn Road. The man in question was Robert Wood, a twenty-nine-year-old artist of Frederick Street, Gray's Inn Road. He had been employed by the same firm, the Sand Blast Glass Company, for fourteen years. Neil introduced himself and said he needed to speak to Wood. Neil then elaborated:

I have been making certain enquiries respecting the murder of Emily Elizabeth Dimmock at 29 St Paul's Road, Camden Town on the night

Agar Grove, once St Paul's Road, 2006. This was where Bertram Shaw and Phyllis Dimmock lived. Author's collection

of September 12. Some post cards have been found which were sent to her by a man with whom she was acquainted. I have reason to believe that they were written by you and that she was known to you as 'Phyllis'.

Wood replied, 'Yes, quite right: but I only wrote one of them – the one with the sketch of the Rising Sun on it'. Neil then declared that he would have to accompany him to the police station, to which Wood agreed. He calmly said goodbye to his companion, quite certain that he would come to no harm. He told her, 'Goodbye, dear, don't worry, I have to go with these gentleman. If England wants me, she must have me, don't cry, but be true.' 'Leave that to me,' she answered. Wood was more than happy to talk to the police about the situation, which had been worrying him for some time. His elder brother, Charles, had advised him to contact the police over the matter of sending the card to Phyllis, but he had been busy at work, with his boss being away. Wood admitted to having had a brief acquaintance-ship with Phyllis, having spent time with her on the Friday night before the murder. He claimed that he knew very little about the murder that would help solve it and said, 'If one has a good name, you don't care to be mixed up in matters of this sort.'

Neil then said that the paper found at the scene of the crime was a letter making an appointment with Phyllis at the Eagle public house in Camden on the Wednesday evening and that it was in the same handwriting as the postcard which Wood had sent her. He denied he sent the letter. Even so, there was enough evidence to take Wood before Clerkenwell Magistrates' Court on the charge of murder, and he was remanded in custody, the plea for bail having been refused.

Meanwhile, the inquest was taking place. It soon transpired that Wood had not been as honest as he had liked to appear. Mrs Ellen Lawrence said Wood had known Phyllis for fifteen months. She had seen Phyllis on the Monday before the murder and thought she was afraid of Wood. Florence Smith agreed with the latter supposition and said that Phyllis and Wood had been together on both 6 and 9 September at the Rising Sun. Other witnesses also attested to the fact that Wood and Phyllis had often been seen together in the streets and in public houses. However, William Lineham said that the man Phyllis was frightened of was not Wood but a Scotsman, whom Phyllis referred to as 'Jock'. Gladys Lineham referred to this mystery man as Scotch Jack, who had 'threatened to do her in'.

Perhaps more importantly, Phyllis and Wood were together at the Eagle on the evening of 11 September. Lilian Raven, a barmaid there, said that the two were there at 9.30 and that Phyllis left at about 10.00 pm. She noticed that she had curling pins in her hair. Another man came in to see Wood and Phyllis said to him, 'You really must excuse me for being so untidy, but I had to come and see him'. The man then departed. Wood and Phyllis eventually left together.

But, for Wood, there was worse to come. Robert McGowan, a carman, recalled leaving home in Chalk Farm on the following morning at 4.40 am in search of work. Just before 5.00, he was passing through St Paul's Street and heard footsteps behind him. Turning, he saw a man leaving the house where Phyllis lived. He was wearing a bowler hat and a short, loose overcoat. He walked briskly away. He had a peculiar gait and jerked his shoulders as he walked. McGowan picked Wood out of an identity parade, but only when Wood moved off – McGowan recognised the way he jerked his shoulders. However, although McGowan had passed nearby, he had not seen the man's face and it had been dark. And the man he had seen had been broad, whereas Wood was slimly built.

Then there was evidence about the mysterious 'Scotch Bob'. Mary Campbell had known Phyllis for two years and said that Phyllis had told her that 'Scotch Bob' had threatened 'to do her in' because of what she had done to him (passed on a venereal disease?). On 11 September, Phyllis had told Mary that she had had a letter from this man, asking her to meet him at Camden Town station. She was afraid to meet him, but feared it would be the worse for her if she did not. Then, at 10.00 that night, Mary saw Phyllis near to the Rising Sun and she was trembling. A man wearing a bowler hat and a short overcoat was nearby (this sounds like the man McGowan later described as the killer) and this was the man referred to as 'Scotch Bob'. The couple walked off and the last Mary saw of Phyllis was at 11.00 pm by the music hall in Euston Road. John Crabtree, a brothel owner, said that about a year before, when Phyllis lodged at his place, she was being threatened with a razor by a man, known as 'Scottie', who also hit her. Yet could the term 'Scotch Bob' refer to Wood – after all, his father was Scottish and Robert can be shortened to Bob?

The inquest was concluded. Witnesses spoke in the defence of Wood. Joseph Lambert recalled seeing Wood on 11 September, but he was wearing a blue suit, not an overcoat. William Moss, a colleague, attested that he had known Wood for some months, but had never seen him in a dark overcoat. He had seen him at work at 8.00 am on the 12 September and that his demeanour was perfectly ordinary, as it was on subsequent days. Charles Wood gave a character reference, claiming his brother was respected by all and was the gentlest of men. He said his brother did not contact the police earlier about the postcard, but their father was unwell and the shock might damage his health. George Wood, Robert's father, a seventy-year-old printer, with whom he lived (in Frederick Street, not far from St Paul's

Road), said that his son returned home at midnight on 11 September. Wood's stepbrother, Joseph, who also lived with him, thought Wood returned at 11.20 pm on that night.

The coroner summed up and told the jury that Wood and Phyllis had been together at the Eagle on 11 September and that he had written a postcard to her, the handwriting being the same as that of a letter arranging to meet her on that evening. Wood had been identified as the man leaving her flat on the following morning, though the identification was possibly open to question. Wood might have committed the murder in a state of frenzy, or perhaps due to jealousy or vengeance. The jury agreed that there was sufficient evidence against Wood that he should stand trial for Phyllis's murder.

Wood was again brought before the magistrates on 6 November. The two main pieces of evidence against him, according to Sir Charles Matthews, who was leading the case against him, were the postcards, which Wood sent to her on 9 September, and the letter arranging to meet her on the 11th. There were a number of other postcards in the flat, stuck into a postcard album, but some had been removed, probably recently and probably by the killer, in order to remove evidence which might incriminate him. The postcard sent by Wood had not been placed in the album yet – it had been put into a drawer in the chest of drawers and so remained to be found.

Wood came to write and send the postcard in the following manner. He had met Phyllis on 6 September at the Rising Sun. A street seller of postcards arrived in the pub and Phyllis asked Wood for one. He obliged and promised to send her one. Roberts, a ship's cook, spent 9 September with Phyllis and she showed Wood's card to him. On the morning of the 11th, she received two letters and Roberts testified that one requested a meeting with her that night at the Eagle. Roberts was shown both and thought that the handwriting was the same. However, Phyllis then destroyed the letters, and only a few unburnt fragments remained.

It was also discovered that Wood was on friendly terms with one Ruby Young. The two had been on intimate terms for some years, but had fallen out over Wood seeing other women earlier that year. On the day after seeing an account of the murder in the newspapers, Wood contacted Ruby. They met and he asked her to lie on his behalf and to say that she was with him on 9 and 11 September. Clearly he anticipated being arrested for the murder. Ruby agreed. Yet crucially, on the night of the murder, he asked her only to say that she had been with him on the evening of the 11th – whereas the murder had been committed in the early hours of the following day. The real killer would have known this and so have asked for an alibi for those hours. Wood did not. Thus he was probably not the killer. Wood also asked his colleague, Lambert, not to say he had seen him with Phyllis. Another of Wood's colleagues recognized the handwriting from a newspaper, but Wood begged him to say nothing on the grounds that it would hurt his aged father, who was ill. The discussion between Wood and his elder brother was also alluded to. It was looking very black against Wood.

Wood stood trial for his life at the Old Bailey on 12 December. This attracted widespread publicity and was much talked about throughout the country and in the colonies, partly because of the horrific nature of the death of a young woman but also because of the apparently attractive character of the accused. The trial lasted several days, and all the major witnesses talked at length, mostly repeating what they had already said. Wood pleaded 'not guilty'. One of the key witnesses for the prosecution, McGowan, was ridiculed by Edward Marshall Hall, who was acting for Wood, asking, after he said that the man he saw was broad, which Wood was not, 'Would you describe a bluebottle as being bigger than an elephant because it was bigger than a fly?' A notable feature of the trial was that Hall put his client in the witness box to speak on his own behalf, the first time that this had ever happened in an English court.

Another development was the discovery of the identity of the mysterious Scot. He was Alexander Mackie, employed as a kitchen

The Central Criminal Court, c.1900. Scene of Robert Wood's trial. Author's collection

porter at Portpatrick Hotel in Wigtonshire from 6 June until 15 September 1907. He was sleeping on the premises on 11 September. He was clearly not the killer.

A week later, the trial came to an end. The judge told the jury that, although no motive had been suggested why anyone should kill Phyllis, it was not their duty to look for reasons why. Many murders, he said, had been committed without any obvious motive. The judge said that he thought Wood had been living a double life – on the one hand he was a trustworthy employee and good fellow, on the other, he was in the habit of resorting with prostitutes. Circumstantial evidence, though, was stacked against him. Apart from McGowan's evidence, there was nothing even to hint that Wood had been with Phyllis on the morning of the murder. However, he had told lies and asked others to lie on his behalf. He thought that the jury ought to give Wood the benefit of the doubt. This they did, and Wood was discharged.

Was Wood innocent, or was he lucky? He might have written other postcards to her and these were the ones he removed from the postcard album, not finding the one he had sent her most recently. Perhaps he wanted to resume his relationship with Ruby and so killed Phyllis lest she object and make life difficult for him. He certainly had seen her on the night of the murder and at other times. Was Wood the man McGowan saw – assuming he was the killer? Possibly. The case against him is certainly a strong one and the lies he told made an unfavourable impression, too. Yet, as said, he asked Ruby to cover him for the evening before the murder, not its actual time.

The police thought he was guilty. Inspector Neil later wrote, after Wood had been discharged:

The case was a most difficult and complicated one and the coolness exercised by the murderer, whoever he might have been was most remarkable and, as must be admitted, this made my task a very arduous one . . . Although we must abide by the jury's decision, there is no moral doubt that Wood was guilty of the murder.

Yet it could not be certain that he was the killer. Phyllis had many associations with men and any one of them might have killed her. Prostitution is a dangerous and secretive business as Dora Piernick, Alice McKenzie, Emma Jackson, Harriet Buswell, Esther Praager and Frances Coles also discovered to their cost. Some commentators have opined that the killings of Dora, Phyllis and Esther were linked, as the killings all occurred within five years and in districts not too distant. Certainly Sir Melville Macnaghten thought so. Henry Adams in about 1914 pointed out the difficulty of solving such murders:

These murders of prostitutes are nearly always of a baffling nature, must necessarily be on account of the nature of the circumstances preceding and surrounding them. The whole business is carried out in secrecy, and the victim assists her own slayer to escape by the manner which she makes his acquaintance and smuggles him into her room. She is unconsciously privy to her own demise and baffling the ends of justice.

It was probably some man who had known her for some time – and who had sent her postcards, which he removed after the murder. In detective fiction, Shaw would be a strong suspect, killing Phyllis for continuing her old way of life after all he had done for her – providing her with a home and a small weekly income. Yet he could not possibly have been guilty as he was out of London at the time. Nor could Alex Mackie be guilty as he was at the hotel in Scotland at the time of the murder, although one of Phyllis's friends thought he was hanging about on 11 September. Perhaps there was another man in Phyllis's murky past. The fact that she was afraid of some man points to this being a likely hypothesis, but who? This must have been the man she had to meet at the railway station – which clearly was not Wood as she had already met him at the Eagle. Remember that she had had two letters and the contents of one are unknown. Assuming Wood wrote her the one about the meeting in the pub, he would hardly have written her another. Was this one from her real killer? But if so, why did the two go back to her room, as presumably she would only have taken back someone she trusted. Unless he promised her he had changed his ways? The questions which need answers are many and are likely to remain imponderables.

A book about the murder ends with an intriguing brief encounter between Marshall Hall and an unnamed man outside a provincial assize court a few years later. A small, happy man approached the barrister and said, 'I see you don't know me, Sir Edward'. 'No, I'm afraid I don't. Please forgive me. I have a terrible memory for faces . . . But, why, isn't your name Wood – Robert Wood?' 'No, its not, but I'd like you to know I'm doing very well, and I owe it all to you'. Was this man Wood? If so, was he thanking Hall for having got him off and saving him from the rope? Or perhaps it was someone totally unconnected with the case.

In recent years, Patricia Cornwell, a best-selling crime novelist, has proposed the theory that Walter Sickert (1860–1942), a Bohemian artist, killed Phyllis, as well as being Jack the Ripper, although this is almost wholly based on surmises. If Sickert was a prostitute killer, it is curious that Cornwell does not accuse him of killing Dora Piernicke or Esther Praager. He painted a picture titled *The Camden Town Murder* based on this crime in 1909 and it is suggested he drew from first-hand experience. The picture shows a clothed man and the naked Phyllis on the bed. However, there is no evidence that Sickert even knew Phyllis and no one mentioned his name in connection with her. Sickert was probably in France at the time. It seems highly unlikely he was the culprit, either. As with many theories about the Ripper, this appears to be yet another case of a writer choosing a suspect – almost always someone well known – and then selecting evidence to make him fit the crime.

Another theorist suggests that George Stocks, who worked on the railways and lived in the same building, may have killed her. He normally left for work at 5.00 am, but on the day of the murder did not do so, apparently having overslept. The same writer suggests, alternatively, that a woman killed Phyllis – could this have been Ruby, who was in love with Wood and so killed her rival? Finally, the man whom McGowan saw need not have been the killer, and the murderer might have left by another exit apart from the front door. These theories are possible, but can only remain as unproven hypotheses.

CHAPTER 23

The 'Very Nervous' Man in the Public Toilets
1908

There are, however, homicidal maniacs – and worse – abroad in this great city and, at rare intervals, some hapless child falls into their hands.

On Friday afternoon, 30 May 1908, Marie Ellen Bailes, a six year old, left the school she attended, St John's Catholic School, in Islington. Marie lived with her parents at Prebend Road, Islington, and she had had lunch there between 1.00 and 2.00 pm and had happily returned to school, which was about twenty minutes walk away. She was told not to dawdle and to 'look sharp home'. Yet she failed to return. Alfred, her father, who was employed in a gutta-percha factory, searched Highbury Fields and other places where she might have been and, failing to find her, notified the local police. It is unknown what happened to her in the few hours after she left school.

Next morning, on the other side of London, William Joseph Votier, the lavatory attendant at St George's Street, Southwark, noticed a man enter the lavatory carrying a brown parcel and who was apparently in 'a very nervous state'. The man seemed very concerned with his curious luggage. The attendant had his own work to perform, and momentarily forgot about the man. After a while, though, his thoughts returned to him.

The strange man had left, but had not taken his parcel away with him. Votier removed the parcel to his office, and, given its odd touch and appearance, decided to open it. But after he had cut the string, which bound it, he received a shock. Wrapped in a blanket was the corpse of a young girl, lacking any clothes. She had been horribly mutilated, so much so that one newspaper described this as 'Fiendish Ripper Crime in South London'. The blanket also contained a quantity of sand; perhaps the corpse had been buried in sand at some time?

The police were then called and the corpse was taken to Southwark Mortuary. Bailes was summoned and he sadly identified the corpse as that of his daughter. He said, 'She was a lovely child, and a bonny girl, almost too big for her age'. The lavatory attendant was able to supply a description of the 'nervous man' who had brought a parcel with the grisly content into the lavatories, as follows:

> . . . about thirty-three years of age, about five feet six inches, or five feet seven inches in height, and of slight build, and with a fair complexion. His face is said to be clean-shaven with the exception of a light brown moustache, and the hair is also of a light brown colour. He wore a dark tweed jacket and a vest, dark tweed cap and dark grey trousers, with a double linen collar and a dark sailor knot-tie.

The blanket was also described, as being seven feet two inches by five feet six inches, with two blue outer lines and two yellow inner ones. The centre was red, much darned and worn and the red stitching was completely off one end.

An arrest was soon made by the Derbyshire Police. They took one Llewellyn Pendrigh, a painter of Marlborough Street, London, into custody on the day after the corpse had been discovered. Pendrigh had travelled northwards from London on the day of the discovery of the crime, and could not account for his movements on the day of the murder. He seemed to resemble the wanted man and had a razor on his person. Yet when he was shown to Votier, he was not recognized and so was released.

The inquest was held on Tuesday 3 June. It was noted that there was a parcel of clothing near the river bank and the initial conjecture was that these belonged to the killer, who removed them before drowning himself in the Thames. Yet this theory was discounted.

Bailes was the first witness. He said that his daughter was not shortsighted, so would not have gone off with someone under the presumption it was someone she knew. Thomas Bone, a schoolboy aged eleven, said that he had seen Marie on Friday. She was at the bottom of Packington Road with a girl called Kirsch. Thomas said Marie told him that she was going home – she was only a dozen houses away, and was going to run because she was late and her brother was about to come home. Kirsch claimed she did not walk home with Marie, but Thomas was adamant on this point.

Votier was the most important witness. He said he had first seen the unknown man at 8.45 standing outside a boot shop. He had gone down the stairs with difficulty with his heavy parcel and had asked Votier to open a cubicle for him. Ten minutes later the man was gone and Votier said he would know him again, if he saw him.

Dr Henry then gave the medical evidence. He had seen the corpse at 9.25 am on the day of its discovery. The little body had been bundled up, tied in this fashion by a piece of rope. Death was due to the throat being cut and there was an additional cutting wound on the chest. A very sharp instrument would have been needed to make these cuts. There was also a bruise behind the left ear, where she had perhaps been stunned before being killed. He thought that death had occurred between about 6.00 and 9.00 pm the previous evening. The doctor also noted that there was sand in the corpse's nostrils, mouth, ears and eyes. The wounds contained some of the same substance. Presumably the body had been temporarily covered with some sandy soil, unless the murder took place in a playground with a sand pit.

Henry concluded by remarking that the girl had probably been stunned before she had been killed, and that the chest wound was probably caused after death. She had been tied up after death, too. She had not been sexually molested. It was impossible to tell if she had had any sweets as she had had a hearty meal earlier in the day and any sweets would have dissolved. Marie may have been enticed away by a stranger with the offer of sweets.

After the doctor had finished, an unknown man decided to address the court. He said that he wished to ask Henry two important questions. He was allowed to do so. The man stated that he had been trying to draw the attention of the police to atrocities committed on children for the past twenty-five years. The coroner wanted to shut him up, as he was not on the jury and so was not allowed to speak at this stage of the inquiry. The man would not shut up and asked about any blood in the corpse's throat. He was interrupted again. Finally the coroner ordered that the inquest be adjourned. The mysterious man was seen talking to the jury and on his way out, he shouted, 'I have done all I wanted to do, I have told the jury.'

There were a number of possible leads. A man had been seen in Kennington Park with a child. One Mr Harmshar, a shopkeeper, recalled selling brown paper for wrapping a parcel at his stationer's shop on High Street, Barnet, on the night of the disappearance, to a man who fitted the description of the killer. But there were many similar stories from all over London, and none of these came to anything. Nor were the clothes ever found, although there was an unfounded rumour that they had been located at the corner of Vincent Terrace and Colebrook Row in Islington.

On 8 June, a man was taken to Wandsworth Police Station and questioned on this matter. Apparently he had turned up at Wandsworth workhouse a few days earlier. Officials there had noticed spots of blood on his clothing and he resembled the man whom Votier

Elephant and Castle, c.1900s. The killer probably took a train from Islington here, before disposing of the corpse. Author's collection

described. However, it was discovered that he knew nothing of the matter.

The police worked hard but without success. They spoke to hundreds of people both north and south of the Thames. The sand found with the corpse was analysed and London was searched for similar substances. All this was to no avail. Sir Melville Macnaghten later wrote:

> *Police were working in the dark from the outset, and never saw a ray of daylight in the case at all. Here was a child of about eight years of age, stopped in the busy street by someone, taken somewhere to enclosed premises of some sort, done to death, and then wrapped up in a parcel and carried right across London [four and a half miles] . . . But we were hopelessly baffled and not the slightest clue was ever vouchsafed to us.*

The girl's killer was never caught. Why had he committed this foul deed? There is no apparent motive – as the sexual one can be discounted. Macnaghten noted: 'There are, however, homicidal maniacs – and worse – abroad in this great city and, at rare intervals, some hapless child falls into their hands.' The murder may have been committed in Islington. Presumably he decoyed the girl away by some method and then killed her, perhaps for the mere sadistic pleasure that the act caused him. He then concealed the corpse and disposed of it some distance from the scene of the crime. He probably did not live alone and so could not have kept it where he lived. The killer could then have taken it in a parcel on the train from the Angel to the Elephant station on the City and South London Railway. Clearly there was a risk of his being stopped and searched, but this was probably minimal. He took a further risk in disposing of the corpse where he did, as Votier had been able to give a good description of him to the police. He could have dumped the corpse in a more remote place where no one would have seen him. Be that as it may, this homicidal maniac escaped into the great metropolis.

Chapter 24

The Death of a Polish Prostitute (2) 1908

It is true that he was never found, and so far as his identity was concerned, it was of course, a mystery.

The young Esther Praager, a Jewess, was only fourteen when she moved with her brother from Warsaw to London in 1905. She initially went to stay with her married sister, Selina Cooper, who lived in East London Street. Here she stayed rent free. Esther did not know a word of English when she arrived, but picked up the language whilst she was with the Coopers, and she earned her living by making blouses and trying her hand at two other trades.

After about eighteen months, Esther decided that there must be more to life than this. Furthermore, she had a row with her sister. Her brother-in-law, Julian Cooper, a chemical dealer, decided that she would have to go. However, he made her an allowance of 2 shillings a week for lodgings elsewhere. He also tried to find her work, but to no avail. Esther made her living by walking the streets, despite all Selina's efforts to convince her otherwise, even to the extent of following her and arguing with her, up to 16 October 1908. Esther was known by her fellows as 'Die Kleiner' (the little one) on account of her being only five feet in height.

She did have one long-term companion. This was Mark Hert, a waiter of Umberton Street, near to the Commercial Road. The two had met in June in a dance hall. They had lived in Leeds and Birmingham as husband and wife in the summer of 1908, but had not lived together in London.

In September and October 1908, Esther resided at a house in Devonshire Street. Alice Riley, stated as being a dressmaker, who also lived there, recalled that on about 10 October, there was a quarrel because Esther would not let a man stay there, and he said he would 'get his own back'. He was a short man and had a moustache. Esther also told her cousin, Mrs Fanny Todan, of a man who wished to be revenged upon her. In any case, Esther did not stay there much longer, being asked to leave by the landlady on 16 October. By 3.00 pm in the afternoon, she had left, Hert taking her box, but she did not tell him where she was moving to, only hinting at the West End.

From 6.00 pm that evening, Hert was at work in the restaurant until the following morning. In fact, Esther had moved to a room on the second floor of a house in Bernard Street, Russell Square, which had been conveniently vacated earlier that week by a Mrs Margaret Harris (a fellow prostitute) who recommended Esther to Mrs Emily Cook, the housekeeper there. That evening, Esther arrived with a hat box and a boy carrying her trunk. Calling herself Mrs Smith, she paid a week's deposit of 15 shillings and received her street key. According to Inspector Stockley, who later saw the room, 'Everything indicated that she had gone to bed in the ordinary manner. The street door-key was on the mantelpiece with other articles, including an empty purse.'

Esther left the house that night to ply her trade. Ange Moltzmer said that she was with her from 9.30 to 10.30 pm, before they went towards Russell Square. It was there that they met a young man. This would appear to be the same man as was later seen with Esther. Mrs Harris saw her at 11.30 pm at the corner of Guildford Street near the

Russell Square, c.1909. Esther Praager was seen with a man here, shortly before her death. Author's collection

Hotel Russell. Esther was with a young man. He was about twenty-four or twenty-five and was short (a little under five feet). He was clean-shaven, pale and had broad features. He wore a cap, a dark grey suit, the jacket of which was buttoned and the collar was low. Generally speaking, he presented a shabby appearance, but walked sharply and was broad shouldered. Although Esther told Mrs Harris that she was going to bed, the man said nothing; perhaps in order to conceal his accent, for his nationality was unknown. This may have been the same man as the one whom Alice Riley said had threatened Esther earlier. They went in the direction of Bernard Street.

At about midnight Esther and her companion went to George Lupitza's, a grocer's shop in Vernon Place, to buy sandwiches.

At 11.45 pm that night, Mrs Cook went to bed, sleeping in the basement. She was tired and slept easily, without anything disturbing her. She rose at 7.00 am on the Saturday morning of 17 October. Going up to the second floor, she noticed that Esther's door was closed. About five hours later, a lodger who had the front rooms spoke to her. She said that she had heard screams at about 2.00 am in the morning, but she did not think that they came from anyone in the house.

But there was fresh cause for anxiety that evening. Another lodger, a young man, returned from work and asked Mrs Cook about the disturbance of the previous night. When she explained that she did not know what he was talking about, he told her that he had heard screams in the house. Mrs Cook then went to see Mrs Rose, the owner of the house, who lived in Marchmont Street. She sent her son, Arthur Chapple, a marine engineer, to investigate.

The two arrived at the house. Chapple went into Esther's room, the blinds of which were still down, and the door unlocked, though closed. Mrs Cook followed with a candle. Apparently, 'The bed was in great disorder and the clothes were heaped up at the foot. Mr Chapple removed a portion of the sheets and a towel from the heap'. It was then that Mrs Cook saw Esther's face. She appeared to be dead, so Mrs Cook set off for the police station.

She did not have to go that far. In the street, PC Mark March was on hand. Mrs Cook said to him, 'I believe a woman has been murdered upstairs'. March went with her and confirmed that this was so. Dr James O'Donnell was summoned and arrived at 7.30 am. Esther was lying on her back and O'Donnell removed the sheeting from her. Although a towel had been knotted and wrapped around her neck, this had been done after death. He also noticed a piece of red insulated wire, of the type used by electricians, lying against the right side of the neck. There were other pieces of similar wire in the room. It seemed possible that these had been brought by the killer

Bernard Street, 2006. Esther's body was found in a room in this street in 1908.
Author's collection

either to tie up his victim or to strangle her. There were knots in both the wires and the towel around her neck. These were granny knots, allegedly favoured by sailors, but in fact the easiest and simplest knots of all to make. The water in the basin in the room was dirty, probably where the killer washed his hands.

Esther was only wearing a chemise, which was stained with blood. There were a number of injuries to her face and neck, and a wound on her right breast. She had been dead for about sixteen or eighteen hours, so must have been killed between about 1.00 and 3.00 am that morning. Death was due to suffocation, perhaps by a human hand. The scratching around the neck indicated that Esther had resisted her attacker. There had probably been a fierce struggle before death, as the mattress and the sheets in the room had been torn.

At the inquest, one Maurice Dubin recalled smoking in his room in the same house. At about a 1.45 am that morning he heard a muffled noise, like a scream, but he thought that it was far away, as if someone was drunk and fighting in the street. He heard a voice cry out 'Ga volt', which is an appeal for help, and then 'Police'. Such noises that he heard only lasted a few minutes and then he thought no more about them. His wife, Sophia, also thought she heard screams. Lesley Wade, a clerk, thought he heard someone's name being cried out but could not remember it.

An unnamed witness later said that he saw a man leave the building at 3.30 am that morning. Was this a man leaving early for work or was it the murderer?

The police had divergent views on the crime. Chief Inspector Thomas Divall wrote:

> *Personally I took no active part in the Praager murder, but after reading the reports I formed the opinion that the murder had been pre-meditated and that the motive for the crime was jealousy. There was not the slightest doubt that it was neither lust nor robbery, and though the victim was a prostitute, she had what is known as a ponce, or a man who lives on a woman's prostitution. He had an idea that another man of his class was gaining her affection.*

Chief Inspector Arrow thought otherwise:

> *There was no mystery at all about this case. The man who committed the murder was undoubtedly the man who was seen in the company of the deceased woman and who purchased the sandwiches for her. It is true that he was never found, and so far as his identity was concerned, it was of course, a mystery. As to his motive, the probability is that they had a quarrel about money matters, words led to blows, which culminated in murder.*

Either of these theories is possible. But it seems more likely that Esther was killed by the short young man who was her final client. He probably planned the murder – hence the bringing of the wires to use against her. It is probable that he was the same man who had quarrelled with her a few days before the murder. Perhaps he had convinced Esther with arguments, monetary or otherwise, that he no longer wished to harm her. Fatally, she had believed him and took her back to his room. Had her lover, Hert, not had a strong alibi, he would have been a major suspect, but as it was, he was in the clear.

Chapter 25

An Actor's Final Curtain 1910

Police were completely baffled. The bottom was knocked out of every workable theory.

Edward Noice, a motor-car driver of Rosenau Road, Battersea, was strolling on that same road on the evening of 16 July 1910. It was about 9.30 pm. He heard a couple of shots ring out in quick succession. Immediately afterwards, a man broke through the gardens of nearby Cambridge House, after having climbed over the wall of a nearby property. He then ran down Rosenau Road in the direction of Petworth Street, towards the Thames. Noice noticed that the man was about five feet six inches in height and was not wearing an overcoat. He did not appear to be a labourer. Nothing else in his appearance registered in Noice's mind. The latter was clearly a good citizen. He went to the nearest police station and reported what he had heard and seen only five minutes after it had happened.

Sergeant Buckley accompanied Noice to Clifton Gardens, Prince of Wales Road, where the man had been seen leaving. Buckley tried to gain entry to the ground floor flat of the building in question. No one seemed to be at home. He then tried the door of the first floor flat. His knocking was answered by Miss Elizabeth Earle, the flat's occupant (writers in the 1920s and 1930s coyly referred to her as Miss Blank or Miss X or said her name was unimportant). Buckley explained his task to her, 'I have received information that two shots have been fired at the rear of these premises. Will you allow me to come through and make a search?' She replied, 'Yes, I heard the shots fired and saw a man climb over the wall.'

As Buckley was walking through the kitchen to gain access to the rear, he met Thomas Frederick Anderson, a twenty-one-year-old warehouseman of Wood Street, who had been with Miss Earle in the flat. He accompanied the policeman as they went down the iron staircase which led from the flat to the back garden.

Prince of Wales' Gardens, Battersea, 2006. Thomas Anderson was shot in a garden behind this street. Author's collection

The two men searched the garden. Buckley examined the wall which the man had climbed over. Anderson was about to remount the stairs when he saw something on the steps leading to the scullery of the first floor flat. He called over to Buckley,

'There's a man lying here'.

Buckley investigated and saw there was the body of a man, lying on his back, with his legs stretched out towards the yard, just where Anderson had indicated. The latter then fetched a light and Buckley took a closer look.

The man had a small bullet wound on the right-hand side of the face, just beneath the nose. He was bleeding and unconscious. Buckley then turned the man's head and saw another bullet wound, this time on the temple. His eye was hanging out over his left cheek. The man was fully clothed, but wearing only slippers on his feet. Buckley asked Anderson, who did not see the corpse clearly, but was given a verbal description, if he knew who he was, and he answered in the negative. Miss Earle, who came down the stairs, did not seem to be agitated.

Inspector Geake had been informed at the police station at 9.45 pm that a man had been shot, so he summoned the divisional surgeon, Dr Kempster. Geake took four constables and an ambulance to the premises. No one was allowed to leave or enter. Anderson said he needed to return home by 11.30 pm, but was not permitted to do so. He felt sick. Buckley then took him to one side and asked him if he had ever heard of anyone called Atherton. He said he had not, but had known of a man called Atherstone.

Another detective showed him a business card with that name on it, which had been found on the corpse and it was only then that the grim truth sunk in. He replied, 'That's my father's card'. The police took him to the station, pending enquiries.

Meanwhile, there were a number of possible clues. The police discovered a pair of clean boots wrapped in brown paper, in the empty ground floor flat. At the station, Anderson identified them as being his father's. The corpse was then searched and the following were found. First, a latch-key, which fitted the front door of the first floor flat. Second, there were a number of letters addressed to one Weldon Anderson Esq. of Percy Street, London WC. Thirdly, there was a small notebook, which had had the business card in it. This was a diary and showed that Anderson, who was Miss Earle's lover, was a jealous man. Finally, and perhaps most sinister, in the man's hip pocket was a length of insulated electric cable, some seventeen inches long.

The young man still had some difficulty in comprehending that his father was indeed the man who had been shot dead. He asked if this was the case. Buckley replied, 'I don't know; you will hear'. 'Has he got a false moustache on?' 'No, he is clean shaven'.

Anderson still resisted the inevitable conclusion. 'I can't think it is my father.' 'I don't know, I want you to realize that you are detained for inquiries to be made and nothing else at present.' Anderson's emotions then took over and he burst into tears, and said, 'Good God, it is my father.' Later he said, 'Good God, I saw my father die.' On the following day he officially identified the body at Battersea Mortuary.

Back at the flat, Detective Inspector Badcock discovered two parts of a bullet in a sink in the empty flat – one of the shots had passed through a glass panel of the back door and hit it. Miss Earle was in a state of nervous collapse. She trembled in every limb and complained of the cold. Perspiration ran from her ashen face. She was given brandy and told how an accident two years before had made Anderson jealous. Eventually, Badcock interviewed Miss Earle, who had important information to relate.

Miss Earle was a professional teacher at the Academy of Dramatic Art and had lived at her current address for some years. She had also known the dead man intimately. He was Thomas Anderson, an actor, whose stage name was Weldon Atherstone. He lived at Great Percy Street and had been separated from his wife for many years (she was an Irishwoman and now lived in Dublin). Miss Earle had known him for about eight years since they met on a theatrical tour. He often visited her and usually stayed the night. She had lived in the ground floor flat in about 1900–1906, and at the upper floor flat since then. In 1906, in the former place, her flat had been burgled.

She then recounted the evening's events. Thomas Frederick Anderson, one of her lover's sons, had arranged to meet her at her flat at about 8.30 pm. This was agreeable to her as she said, 'I have known him since from a boy and he had always visited me'.

At first they sat in the sitting room, talking. At 9.00 pm, she showed him some of the new decorations in the bedroom and then they went to the kitchen to have supper. It was then that they heard the two shots.

They went to the door to the back steps and opened it. A man was seen climbing the wall. Miss Earle said that she had wanted to investigate, but the young Anderson persuaded her not to and they resumed their meal, allegedly thinking that someone was shooting at either cats or at burglars, of which there had been many in the locality in recent times. The next they knew of it was when Buckley arrived at the front door.

Miss Earle then told about her relations with the elder Anderson. She had last seen him seven weeks before at the flat and his elder son had been with him. Relations had been amicable. However, eight weeks before that, the two had rowed and Anderson had hit her. Apparently he was a jealous man and accused her of seeing someone else. He had pointed to the sofa and said that the marks on it were proof that someone else had slept there. He said, 'It's all over', and left. This was not the first instance of his jealousy – a year before, Miss Earle had had to stop having male pupils because he thought she might be having an affair with one of them. He left his latch-key to the flat, which she had given him, and asked for any mail for him to be forwarded. Despite his behaviour, Miss Earle would have taken him back. She said, 'I know no one who has any ill-feeling against him. I was more like a mother to his boys, the elder of whom I have taken great interest in and instructed.'

The police had found footprints outside, going towards the flat and away from it, but these did not correspond to the boots belonging to Anderson which had been found in the flat. Nor did they match his elder son's. They might have been made by a man wearing pumps. Meanwhile, Noice was shown the younger Anderson and Noice said that this was not the man he had seen running down the street. He carefully examined the youth and saw that his hands and clothes were clean. Anderson still doubted that his father was dead and again asked if the corpse had had a false moustache as he was surprised that the

Rosenau Road, 2006. The killer of Thomas Anderson fled down here. Author's collection

corpse was clean-shaven. He was asked about the evening and his story corresponded with that already given by Miss Earle.

At the inquest on 24 July, there was further evidence given. Two more witnesses, who had seen the running man, came forward. Mrs Emma Lewis of Juer Street, a housekeeper, had been walking from Battersea Park Road and heard the shots. She saw the man come down from the wall, not far from her. He was about five feet three inches in height and was wearing a dark jacket suit, which was dirty. He was bare handed and had nothing in either. She thought that he was running for assistance. Arthur Jones of Isis Street, a salesman, also thought the man was running to find a doctor, following an attempted suicide by another. He caught a brief glimpse of his face. It was clean-shaven, except, perhaps, for a very fair moustache. He wore a cap and light boots, which did not make a sound. The man seemed more like a clerk than a labourer, and was about twenty-seven. He carried nothing.

Dr Kempster then gave the medical evidence. Life had become extinct at 10.20 pm, about fifty minutes after the shooting. Death had been due to coma following concussion and laceration of the brain due to a bullet wound. The other wound had been merely a flesh wound made by the bullet which had been found in the sink of the ground floor flat. There was considerable scorching around each wound, indicating that the shots had been fired at extremely close range. The angles at which the bullets had entered the head were also such that the wounds could not have been inflicted by someone firing from the ladder of the first floor flat. There were also a few superficial wounds, inflicted in the course of a struggle just where the corpse had been found. Marks were found on the corpse's wrists where he was held briefly, and around his mouth, where an attempt had been made to stop him crying out. It must have been a determined attack, as Anderson was not a weak man. It was possible that the gun was Anderson's own and his killer twisted his wrist so the gun fired into Anderson's own head.

William Anderson, Anderson's youngest son, a sixteen-year-old warehouseman, who lived at Wood Street, London EC, gave evidence about his father. He had been staying with his father at Great Percy Street in the two weeks prior to his death. He said that his father did not talk of Miss Earle, nor did he often go to Battersea. William had not seen her for some months because he did not have the time and had not thought of it; his brother was more friendly with her than he was and often visited her. He said he had never seen the piece of cabling before, but recognised the slippers as his father's. He said that his father was worried about work, but was sober and did not possess a revolver. His father had visited Battersea three days before his death and returned early on the following day (which was apparently unknown to anyone else). Finally, his father was not usually in London, being often on tour with a group of fellow actors. This brother had been at a cricket match at Willesden on the day of the murder before returning home.

He also cast some light on his brother's visit to Miss Earle. He was aware of his intended visit, as was his father. When asked about his brother's not recognizing his father's corpse at first, he said that the blood on his face and the fact that he did not expect to see him there might have accounted for that.

The inquest was adjourned and did not reconvene until 17 September, in order that other witnesses could be questioned and so that the police could make further enquiries.

More information was indeed revealed. The younger Thomas Anderson had told his father of his appointment to see Miss Earle. It was thought that his father might have been to the ground floor flat at other times. It was also pointed out that the cabling he had been carrying would have made an effective weapon.

The younger Thomas Anderson then gave his evidence. He claimed to have 'lived on terms of affection with his father, seeing him frequently when he was in London'. He also said that his brother said that their father was expected on the fatal evening, but he himself was unaware of this. He also had no idea why his father was carrying a weapon on the day he died, nor what the true relations between his father and Miss Earle were, nor about his father's jealousy. The late Mr Anderson kept much to himself and confided in no one. But much of his evidence was merely to confirm what Buckley and Miss Earle had already said about their evening in the flat, the gunshots and the discovery of the corpse.

Miss Earle was the next witness to be called. Again, much of her evidence had already been given to the police. It was pointed out to her that the evidence of Anderson's diary suggested that he had been into her flat when she was out after they had argued and had been keeping watch there. She also agreed that when Anderson was jealous he could be in a violent rage. A year before, he had even apparently threatened to cut her throat. This was put down to the fact that he had injured his head in a motor accident. She swore that there had been nothing to cause such jealousy and she had had no male callers nor any male correspondents.

The diary contained little of use; lists of names were given, but enquiries about the people mentioned were inconclusive. At first the phrase 'If he had kept away from the spell of her fatal fascination and remained out of reach, this would never have happened' looked important, but it was discovered to have been taken from a recent magazine, the *Smart Set*. There were the names of four men in the diary, but all were cleared; two were found to be outside London, another was in Canada and another in America. The coroner concluded 'that this case is as mysterious as it was during the first hour it was known to the police'. No gun was ever found – it was probably thrown into the Thames.

The theory that an armed burglar might have killed Anderson was raised. There had been a spate of burglaries in the locality in recent times and guns were easy to procure quite legally. These thieves had often broken into gas meters. Yet the flats would not provide rich pickings and 9.30 on a summer evening was rather early for most burglars to operate.

Although nothing has come to light since, there are a number of questions which the reader might like to consider. First, what were the relations between the younger Thomas Anderson and Miss Earle? His younger brother described him as being on good terms with her and of visiting her regularly. Was he having an affair with her? Like father, like son? Why did he not want her to investigate the shooting? Surely the natural reaction when hearing nearby gunshots is either to see what is happening or to summon help. The two did neither; they carried on their meal together until interrupted by the police. And why did he not recognize his father immediately? His reasons seem inadequate. If this hypothesis is the case, then presumably the man running from the scene of the crime was a hired assassin. Yet this seems very unlikely. Putting oneself into the power of a third party would have been a very unwise policy. It therefore seems unlikely that the younger Anderson was a party in the killing of his father, whatever his relations with Miss Earle. After all, three witnesses saw this running man. He was not a creation.

But why was Anderson himself there? Presumably for the same reason that he had been haunting the locality in recent days/weeks. He was still jealous of Miss Earle and wanted to confirm his suspicions. The weapon which he had armed himself with was presumably so he could attack her 'lover' – unless it was to despatch her, for he had used violence on her in the past and had threatened to kill her. All this seems fairly certain. He entered the ground floor flat and put his boots away, putting on slippers so as not to make a noise when he engaged in his spying and/or as a prelude to a surprise assault. This seems clear.

In that case, who was the running man? Perhaps he was a burglar. There had been a spate of burglaries in the locality, though to arm oneself with a gun seems extreme, though not impossible. Perhaps Anderson saw the man or was seen by him (the latter seems more likely as he did not pull out his weapon) and a struggle ensued in the yard. The burglar found Anderson to be hardy adversary and so felt it necessary to use his gun in order to avoid capture and arrest. He shot Anderson, then fled. Or was the man the lover of Miss Earle? In this case, Anderson might have been lying in wait for him with the gun and the murder was actually a case of self-defence. Anderson might indeed have been ready to use his gun on the man. After all, if the life preserver was the intended weapon, why was it not to hand for ready use, perhaps up his sleeve, for instance? But if the man was her lover, how did Anderson know when he would arrive? Perhaps he had been spying on the house, but if the unknown man was Miss Earle's lover, then why did he come around on a night his mistress was entertaining the young Anderson? A surprise visit? It seems unlikely.

Neither theory seems to fit. As Sir Melville Macnaghten admitted, 'Police were completely baffled. The bottom was knocked out of every workable theory.'

CHAPTER 26

The North London Train Murder
1914

Neither Starchfield nor his wife bears a good character, but, so far as we have gone, there is no evidence to associate them in any way with the crime.

ittle Willie Starchfield lived with his mother in lodgings in Hampstead Road – his parents having separated a few months previously. Unfortunately, an even greater misfortune was to befall the family on Thursday 8 January 1914.

It is worth making a few comments about the lad. He was a little under six years of age, but was of a striking appearance. He had shoulder length dark brown curls. It was not uncommon for him to be sent on errands. He had suffered an accident during Guy Fawkes Night two months previously and so was not then attending school. He had few friends, though his father thought that the previous July an older boy had gone with him to the cinema.

Mrs Starchfield was visiting Mrs Malcolm, a friend, in Soho Square. They were there from about 10.00 am until 2.00 pm in the afternoon. Willie was left at home with the landlady, Mrs Longstaffe. At 12.30 pm, she sent him out on an errand to a couple of shops about 200 yards away. He did as he was bid and brought home some bread from a baker's. Then he was asked to go to Chapman's Bazaar in order to have a 'Furnished Apartments' card changed for an 'Unfurnished Apartments' card. He went out into Hampstead Road with the new card. He never returned.

He was found at 4.30 pm that afternoon. He had been strangled and the body was discovered in a third class carriage on a City-bound train between Mildmay Park and Dalston Junction stations. His body was identified by Mrs Longstaffe. What had happened in the intervening hours? How did he get on board the train? Who did he meet and where did they meet? Why was he killed? His parents appeared to be in the clear as his mother was with her friend and his father was at his lodgings until 3.30 pm. Presumably a stranger must have offered him some inducement to go with him, rather than to return home for lunch, as would have been the natural course of events.

It was thought possible that he could have been taken by omnibus or tram from Hampstead Road to either Chalk Farm or Camden Town station. Although the latter was nearer (being only a mile distant), the former would have been easier to slip onto unnoticed. There were other reasons why Chalk Farm was more likely. There were lavatories on the platform, where concealment prior to boarding was possible. On the other hand, the staff at the barriers to these two stations did not recollect anyone similar to Willie passing through on the Thursday. The Maiden Lane Station was less well manned, but it was further from Hampstead Road.

Was Willie killed before his body was placed on the train or was he killed on the train itself? A guard had performed a quick search of the carriages of the train at 3.30 pm and found nothing then. It was difficult to believe a corpse could have been smuggled on board, but equally, with only two or three minutes travelling time between each station, a murder on a train which might be boarded by someone else any moment was dangerous, even though traffic in the afternoon would be less than at other times.

John Starchfield, the lad's father, was contacted by the police on the following morning. He was a newspaper seller on Tottenham Court Road, but was quite a celebrity in his own right. On 27 September 1912, he had given chase to an Armenian by the name of Stephen Titus, who had just murdered one Esther Towers, and had been shot by him. He had been awarded £50 by the judge and received a grant from the Carnegie Hero Fund. He had been in bed on the day of the murder of his son until 3.30 pm because the bullet wound he had received was still troubling him. Afterwards, he ate and then sold newspapers in the early evening. He had not seen his son for three weeks.

Yet Starchfield had another side to his character than the one known to the public, and which was certainly not heroic. He had often treated his wife badly. Whilst drunk, he had hit her and had also stolen money from her, whilst giving her none. A separation order had been granted to his near suicidal wife in 1909, when Willie was a baby.

The police tried to find anyone who had seen such a distinctive little lad on the Thursday afternoon. An Italian boy said he had seen him in the company of an older boy walking to Camden Town Station.

There was a dearth of clues. The 'apartments' card he had been sent out with was not on his person. If it could be found, perhaps thrown away somewhere, it might present a clue. It seemed that death had been caused by a light cord, which was also nowhere to be found.

A motive for the murder was also obscure. The Starchfields were a poor family. The boy's mother thought that a maniac must be to blame. One theory was that it was a subtle revenge for his father bringing Titus to justice in 1912. The motive could not have been theft and there was no other mark on the body.

The boy must have been taken by someone in Hampstead Road and then gone with them to the railway station. Was the abductor a stranger – but if so, the boy would have resisted, unless he had been offered an inducement. Was he known to him – but if so, who was it – no one had seen Willie with anyone on previous occasions. No one could recollect having seen the boy on the platforms or on the train. The killer could be male or female, young or old, sane or otherwise.

A few days later, there were reports of sightings. A bus driver said that a 'foreign looking' man pushed a boy onto the bus at Kentish Town station and both of them left near Tufnell Park Tube station, but there was no obvious link between that station and the North London line. The time was 3.30 pm, which also seemed rather late. Perhaps more promising was that the conductor on the Hampstead and Charing Cross Railway saw a man with a child slung over his shoulder board the train at Goodge Street, so not far from Hampstead Road, and leave at Camden Town. The man was five feet nine inches and in his early forties.

Shopkeepers in the Hampstead Road were questioned as to the remains of a currant cake which were found in Willie's stomach. It was probable that his abductor persuaded him to go with him or her with such a lure.

The inquest took place nearly a fortnight after the corpse had been found. Both Willie's parents attended, of course. The cause of death was further discussed. Dr Garrett, the police surgeon, thought that there had been a sign of a struggle, due to scratch marks being evident on the neck. Death occurred between about 2.00 and 3.00 pm. Sir Bernard Spilsbury, a famed pathologist, said that the weak condition of the victim meant that he would have died more quickly than a more healthy specimen. Death probably only took a minute after the cord was applied. A signalman had found a piece of cord on the line near Shoreditch station and Spilsbury thought that might have been the weapon.

Evidence was then given as to the movements of the boy's parents. His mother's were verified by her friends whom she had seen on that day, though one Emily Fay said that she had heard her say in a pub two months before that 'she would have to get rid of her boy before she had another child'. His father's were less certain. Jules Labarbe, manager of the lodging house in Hanover Court where Starchfield stayed, said he saw him in the morning there, but as he had been out in the afternoon, he could not vouch for his lodger's whereabouts later, although Starchfield had been ill recently and was staying longer in bed than was usual. However, William Tilly, who shared a room with Starchfield, said that he was still there until at least 3.00 pm, which was when Tilly left the house. Thomas Stickney recalled seeing Starchfield in the house at 2.50 pm. He was seen in Bloomsbury at 4.20 pm.

Chief Inspector Gough described the dilemma of the police:

Neither Starchfield nor his wife bears a good character, but, so far as we have gone, there is no evidence to associate them in any way with the crime, and in fact no witness of any importance has been traced . . . there is no indication of a motive for any other person to have committed the crime . . . Active enquiries are still being pursued in every possible direction. The usual letters invariably received in cases of this kind, making suggestions etc., have reached us, but nothing of a tangible nature has resulted.

George Jackson, a signalman, had a potentially important snippet of information. He told how he had seen, at about 2.18 pm, the train from Chalk Farm pass by his signal box. In a third class compartment, he saw a man leaning over a curly haired child. The man had a dark moustache, a dark bowler hat and a dark coat. He was probably aged over twenty-five. When Jackson saw Willie's corpse at the mortuary, he said that the child he had seen was indeed he. William Morcher, a train driver, said that he saw, at about 2.30 pm, a powerfully built, broad shouldered man in a third-class compartment tying up a parcel.

However, the most dramatic evidence came from Mrs Clara Wood of Kentish Town. At a 1.15 pm, she had been in Kentish Town, outside a drapery shop. She saw a man and a small boy walk from the direction of Camden Town Station. The man was in his late thirties, about five feet two inches in height. He had a dark complexion and a dark moustache and wore a felt hat. He looked like an Italian. The child was eating cake and she recognized who it was from a photograph that was later shown of Willie.

All this was well and good. But the most shocking moment was yet to come. The foreman of the jury then put a question to her, 'Have you seen the man again?' 'Yes'. 'Where?' 'Here' replied Mrs Wood. 'Here' repeated the foreman, 'Where?' Mrs Wood then looked around the court and was silent for some moments as tension mounted. Then she looked at a man who was sitting in the witness box. She pointed her finger at him and said, 'Yes, that is the man, sitting close to that lady'. At which the woman, who was the accused man's wife, cried, 'Oh, don't say that, don't say that'. The accused man sprang to his feet and cried 'Me?'

It was John Starchfield.

Mrs Wood was in no doubt about it, however, and she said, 'Oh it is you. I am sorry, but it is you. This is the second time I have seen you today.' She had seen him outside the courtroom. Starchfield denied it and was, when the court adjourned, allowed to leave, unaccompanied.

In the next few days and weeks, more witnesses came forward against Starchfield. One was a timber porter, called Moore, who had approached a newspaper with his evidence. He said that he saw the two together outside the station. Another was Richard White, a salesman, who said he saw Starchfield and the boy at Camden Town station. He thought they seemed friendly enough together. He had recognized them by their photographs being published in the press.

On the other hand, Fanny Parsons came forward and said that she had seen Willie with a woman on the day of the murder. Reuben Symons said he saw a woman in her early thirties, perhaps a labourer's wife, with a parcel and dragging a child along Camden High Street. A number of railway officials also saw similar sights. Yet Starchfield was accused of the crime at the coroner's and magistrates' courts and so was sent to the Old Bailey for trial.

High Street, Camden Town, c.1910. Was Willie Starchfield seen with a woman in a tram in this street? Author's collection

On 1 April the case came before the judge and jury. The prosecution brought forward its witnesses who identified Starchfield with his son on the afternoon of the murder, but they were shown to be unreliable. Moore was shown to have gone to the newspapers for gain, rather than report his news to the police. More importantly, Moore made mistakes in describing the colour of Starchfield's clothes, claiming they were dark, whereas they were light and that his hat was coloured whereas it was black. The railway employees who had been on duty could not be certain that Starchfield was the man they had seen, either.

The judge questioned whether there was a case for the prosecution. He said:

> *I cannot say, of course, that there is no evidence, because there is evidence of identification, but in a case of this kind, a capital case, you have to put such evidence before the jury as will convince them with certainty that the man has been guilty, or as would leave them with no reasonable doubt in their minds.*

Mr Bodkin, leading the case for the prosecution, agreed with the judge and urged the jury to bring in a verdict of not guilty, which they did. Aspersions were cast on the way in which the coroner's court had operated. There, the police had put questions to the witnesses, often in a leading fashion, when they should have been put by the coroner himself. The collection of signed statements by witnesses was also at fault. To many cheers, Starchfield was released and left the court. Some of the police were still convinced he was the killer; his motive being to cause his estranged wife distress. Yet there is no evidence that he bore any animosity towards his little son (had there been, it would certainly have been used against him, and his wife, who bore him no love, would have been sure to have mentioned it) and to think he could have killed him in order to make his wife suffer seems fantastic.

Starchfield did not have much longer to live. Still troubled by the wound he had received in 1912, he died at St Pancras Infirmary on 20 May 1916 and never spoke of his son's murder. A few weeks previously, a bottle was found in the Thames with a handwritten message inside. It read, 'I, J.S., hereby confess that I murdered my son William in 1914. God forgive me. I deeply regret it. J.S.' However, it must have been a cruel hoax, because the writing did not match that of Starchfield.

In the autumn of that year, one John Fitzpatrick, a porter, confessed. He said that he had taken leave from his job on 7 January 1914 and returned there on the following day. Apparently on the morning of the murder, he drank, then went on a train and was seated in a carriage with several others. When all the adults had left, he was alone

Junction of Hampstead Road and Tottenham Court Road, c.1903. The estranged Starchfields lived in these streets. Author's collection

with Willie. He talked to him and then strangled him, and removed between 10 and 11 shillings from him. The police thought the man was odd, and in any case, the Starchfield family was poor – his mother only had a penny on her at the time of the murder. Willie could not have had the sum quoted on his person. Fitzpatrick was released.

What really happened on that day in North London in January 1914? Almost anyone – man or woman or older child even, could have tempted Willie away with a piece of cake from his errand in Hampstead Road. But why did they want to murder him? Neither sexual perversion nor monetary gain seem to have been the motivating factor. Possibly the killer was suffering from a form of insanity – paranoid schizophrenia is a possibility in the absence of any more tangible motive. Sir Robert Anderson wrote, 'There is the theory of the homicidal maniac. From what I can gather of the facts, I am much inclined to favour this theory.' There seems no reason to dissent from this view. As to the mechanics of the murder, could the boy have been killed before being taken onto the train in a parcel, perhaps, or was he strangled on the train itself? Given the evidence of the signalman, the latter seems likely. Nothing more seems to be reasonably certain. The killer appeared seemingly out of nowhere and disappeared among London's millions just as easily.

Conclusion

There are twenty-five murders chronicled in this book. Those killed were those who were most vulnerable in society – sixteen women, of whom six or seven were prostitutes, five children and four men. The most common murder weapon was a razor or knife in thirteen cases, whilst three victims were strangled, four bludgeoned and one suffocated. Only two were shot and what caused Sarah Snelling's death remains unknown. None were killed by poison – that allegedly classic weapon of the Victorian murderer. But then poisoners were either detected and caught, such as the Deptford mass poisoner in 1889 (whose story is told in the author's *Foul Deeds and Suspicious Deaths in Deptford and Lewisham*) or Crippen two decades later – or they escaped wholly without suspicion. After all, the 'perfect' murder is one which is never even detected as such.

Why the victims were killed is mostly unknown. Two women died because the father of their unborn children wished to cover up his illicit affair. One murder – that of Amelia Jeffs – was due to sexual assault, and some deaths may have been due to robbery, such as that of Robert Westwood and Sarah Snelling. Passion, jealousy or revenge might account for some of these murders. Most of the others are inexplicable, and may have been the result of some form of insanity. Why should anyone kill Willie Starchfield or Eliza Davis?

In all cases, the murderer got away with his crime. And the majority of these undetected killers, if not all of them, were men. Murder is a man's crime, because it usually requires physical strength, and those few female murderers (often poisoners) are viewed as particularly notorious because they are so few. Why did they get away with their crimes? Those addicted to conspiracy theories about Masonic rituals and government cover-ups in the case of the Ripper murders need to see this subject in its wider context. They might like to ask whether any of the murders described here were the result of dastardly conspiracies. None appear to be so. Murders went unsolved partly because the criminal was lucky and competent. They also went unsolved because the police had very primitive techniques at their disposal. It was not that they were necessarily stupid, but they lacked the means to conduct a scientific investigation. In some cases, the police seem to have directed all their efforts towards one suspect or to have not followed up possible leads. And, as has been stated, unsolved murders were a small minority. Finally, juries gave the benefit of the doubt. After all, murder was a hanging offence.

The first lines of this book claimed that a mystery which remains a mystery is an annoyance. It is as if the last chapter had been torn out of a detective novel and the reader does not know whodunit or why. But such is the nature of real life. Life is the unsolved mystery because we will never know how it will end. In this sense, these unsolved murders resemble real life, lacking a neat ending which we may crave. But if the ending were known, would the narrative lose some of its interest? If we knew who killed those unfortunate women in the East End in 1888 (and perhaps beyond), would we be as interested in them and their killer? Probably not. Who now has heard of one of England's worst female serial killers, who killed at least five people for their insurance money in 1889? And who has not heard of Jack the Ripper? Q.E.D.

Appendix

A Partial List of Other Unsolved Murders in London, 1837–1914

1 July 1846	PC George Clarke, Dagenham
14 May 1848	Henry Lazarus, Spitalfields
26 March 1863	Matilda Moore, Bethnal Green
8 November 1863	Mrs Watson, Camberwell
31 January 1869	Samuel Grokett, Regent's Canal
2 April 1869	Nicholas Cambursis, St George's Street
10 July 1872	Sarah Squires and Christina Squires, Hoxton
2 December 1872	Sarah Martin, Hampton
June 1874	Unknown woman in the Thames off Putney
July 1874	Unknown child in the Thames off Vauxhall
13 September 1875	Jane Soper, Borough
18 April 1876	Charles Bravo, Balham
12 February 1877	Joseph Richards, Christian Street
25 March 1877	William Saunders, Penge
11 December 1878	Rachel Samuels, Burton Crescent
1 June 1879	Robert Collins, Rotherhithe
14 October 1879	Matilda Hacker, Euston Square
July 1887	Unknown woman in Regent's Canal
2 April 1888	Emma Smith, Whitechapel
20 August 1888	Torso of an unknown woman found in Whitehall
20 December 1888	Rose Mylett, Poplar
2 June 1889	Elizabeth Jackson, Whitechapel
10 September 1889	Unknown woman in Pinchin Street
4 August 1891	Emily Adams, Limehouse
24 February 1893	Ann Darby
13 May 1893	Fanny Saunders
2 May 1893	Ellen Bance, Victoria Park
31 July 1893	William Goodgin, Westbourne Park
14 November 1894	Alfred Channing, Rushington Street
3 May 1894	James Wells, Barnes
2 July 1895	Florence Ralph, West Ham
12 October 1895	Sidney Dowling, Islington
16 March 1896	Elizabeth Quickfall, Grand Junction Canal
11 April 1896	Frederick St John, Battersea
21 October 1896	PC Michael Ferguson

9 April 1897	Unknown child, Little Marshalsea Street
22 August 1897	Florence Saunders, Peckham
August 1897	Unknown man in the Thames
15 September 1897	William Bennett, Upton
22 October 1897	Mary Marshall, Bethnal Green
27 March 1899	Bertha Russ, West Ham
23 August 1899	Frederick Fisher, Epping Forest
23 November 1899	William Cliff, Yiewsley
3 January 1900	Nicholas Fisher, Drayton Gardens
13 May 1900	Mary Wakeness, Brixton
3 August 1900	Mary Manbridge, Walthamstow
10 October 1900	PC John Schafer, Bethnal Green
1 June 1901	Ann Austin, Spitalfields
9 April 1901	Alfred Hance, Streatham
8 June 1902	Torso of an unknown woman found in Lambeth
1906	Mary Hogg, Camberley
27 August 1907	Rossetta Pook, Leytonstow
14 October 1907	Fortonata Marchesina, Clerkenwell
3 November 1909	Elizabeth Clark, Brixton
21 June 1914	Emily Millard, Grand Junction Canal

This list is by no means comprehensive, and has been mostly drawn up using the National Archives file, reference MEPO 20/1.

In addition there are the victims of Jack the Ripper, killed in Whitechapel and Spitalfields:

7 August 1888	Martha Tabram
31 August 1888	Polly Nichols
8 September 1888	Annie Chapman
30 September 1888	Elizabeth Stride
30 September 1888	Catherine Eddowes
9 November 1888	Mary Jane Kelly

The latter five had their throats cut and all save Stride were mutilated.

Bibliography

Primary Sources

Manuscripts

The National Archives
Metropolitan Police: Murder and Manslaughter Files: MEPO3/40 (Grimwood), 41 (Davis), 42 (Westwood), 55 (Snelling), 57 (Medhurst), 70 (Jackson), 81 (Millson), 82 (Dimmock), 110–15 (Buswell), 118 (Thames body of 1873) 140 (Mckenzie and Coles), 237B and 832 (Starchfield). MEPO20/1 (file listing murders 1890–1912).

Probate Registry (Canterbury)
Will of Robert Westwood.

Principal Registry of the Family Division
Will of Arabella Tyler.
Will of John Maddle.

London Metropolitan Archives
Parish Registers of St Matthew's Yiewsley.

British Library Additional Manuscripts
Correspondence of Rev. Thomas Scott.

Published sources

R Anderson, *The Lighter Side of my Official Life* (n.d.).
Census Returns for 1841–1901.
Chiswick Times (1897).
W Dew, *I caught Crippen* (1938).
T Divall, *Scoundrels and Scallywags* (1929).
S P Evans and K Skinner, *The Ultimate Jack the Ripper Source Book* (2000).
A Griffiths, *Mysteries of the Police and Crime* (1899).
Illustrated Police News (1871, 1880, 1890, 1891, 1894, 1897, 1904, 1908, 1910).
Kentish Mercury (1898).
London Directories.
M Macnaghten, *Days of my Years* (1914).
Middlesex County Times (1897).
W Peacock, *Who committed the Great Coram Street Murder?* (1873).
P Savage, *Savage of Scotland Yard* (1934).

Stratford Express (1882)

The Annual Register (1837, 1838, 1848, 1850, 1857)

The Times (1837, 1838, 1839, 1840, 1848, 1850, 1853, 1857, 1863, 1866, 1871, 1873, 1880, 1889, 1890, 1891, 1894, 1897, 1898, 1904, 1908, 1910, 1914)

F Wensley, *Detective Days* (1931)

West Ham Guardian (1890)

L F Winslow, *Recollections of Forty Years* (1910)

Secondary Sources

H Adam, *The Police Encyclopedia*, vi (*c.*1914).

H L Adam, *Murder by Persons Unknown* (1931).

P Begg and K Skinner, *The Scotland Yard Files* (1992).

B Cobb, *The First Detectives* (n.d.).

R A Downie, *Murder in London* (1973).

C Emsley, *The English Police* (1996).

M Fido, *Murder Guide to London* (1988).

R M Gordon, *The Thames Torso Murders of Victorian London* (2002).

A Lambton, *Echoes of Causes Celebres* (n.d.).

B Lane, *The Murder Club Guide to London* (1986).

F Linnane, *The Encyclopedia of London Crime and Vice* (2003).

T Marriott, *Jack the Ripper: The Twenty First Century Investigation* (2005).

G Mason, *The Official History of the Metropolitan Police* (2004).

D Napley, *The Camden Town Murder* (1987).

J Nash, *Among the Missing* (1978).

E O'Donnell, *Great Thames Mysteries* (1929).

G Sparrow, *Vintage Edwardian Murder* (1971).

W Speer, *The Secret History of Great Crimes* (n.d.).

E Spencer Shew, *A Companion to Murder* (1960).

E Spencer Shew, *A Second Companion to Murder* (1961).

P Sugden, *The Complete Jack the Ripper* (1994).

B Thomson, *The Story of Scotland Yard* (1935).

E Villiers, *Riddles of Crime* (1928).

J R Whitbread, *The Railway Policeman* (1961).

J Wilson, *An Encyclopedia of World Crime* (1991).

Index